Union Public Library
1980 Morris Avenue
Union, N.J. 07083

SCIENCE
FOUNDATIONS

Heredity

Union Public Library
1980 Morris Avenue
Union, N.J. 07083

SCIENCE FOUNDATIONS

The Big Bang
Cell Theory
Electricity and Magnetism
The Expanding Universe
The Genetic Code
Germ Theory
Gravity
Heredity
Natural Selection
Planetary Motion
Plate Tectonics
Quantum Theory
Radioactivity
The Theory of Relativity

SCIENCE FOUNDATIONS

Heredity

KRISTI LEW

An imprint of Infobase Publishing

Heredity

Copyright © 2009 by Infobase Publishing

All rights reserved. No part of this book may be reproduced or utilized in any form or by any means, electronic or mechanical, including photocopying, recording, or by any information storage or retrieval systems, without permission in writing from the publisher. For information contact:

Chelsea House
An imprint of Infobase Publishing
132 West 31st Street
New York NY 10001

Library of Congress Cataloging-in-Publication Data
Lew, Kristi.
 Heredity / Kristi Lew.
  p. cm. — (Science foundations)
 Includes bibliographical references and index.
 ISBN 978-1-60413-042-3 (hardcover)
 1. DNA—Juvenile literature. 2. Genes—Juvenile literature. 3. Heredity, Human—Juvenile literature. I. Title. II. Series.
 QP624.L49 2009
 572.8'6—dc22   2008054310

Chelsea House books are available at special discounts when purchased in bulk quantities for businesses, associations, institutions, or sales promotions. Please call our Special Sales Department in New York at (212) 967-8800 or (800) 322-8755.

You can find Chelsea House on the World Wide Web at
http://www.chelseahouse.com

Text design by Kerry Casey
Cover design by Ben Peterson

Printed in the United States of America

Bang EJB 10 9 8 7 6 5 4 3 2 1

This book is printed on acid-free paper.

All links and Web addresses were checked and verified to be correct at the time of publication. Because of the dynamic nature of the Web, some addresses and links may have changed since publication and may no longer be valid.

Contents

1 An Introduction to Heredity   7
2 Early Ideas about Heredity   16
3 Gregor Mendel: 24
   The Father of Modern Genetics
4 Chromosome Theory of Heredity   38
5 Passing Genes to   47
   the Next Generation
6 When Meiosis Goes Wrong   57
7 Inherited Conditions   71
8 Genetic Medicine   87
9 Genetic Technology   96

Glossary   107
Bibliography   110
Further Resources   115
Picture Credits   117
Index   118
About the Author   122

An Introduction to Heredity

Dogs start out as puppies and kittens turn into cats. Children tend to grow up and resemble their parents and other family members. Passing down traits from parent to child, generation after generation, is called **heredity**. Whether you have black or blonde hair, brown or blue eyes, athletic or musical ability or both, all of these traits are determined, to some degree, by heredity. The question is, how do these traits get passed down?

THE CODE OF LIFE

Cells are the basic building blocks of all living things. There are trillions of cells in the human body, almost all of which contain a chemical molecule that carries hereditary material. This chemical molecule is called **deoxyribonucleic acid**, or DNA. The DNA molecule is usually found in a cell's nucleus, which acts as the command center for the cell, telling the cell when to grow, divide, or die.

Information contained in the DNA molecule tells cells how they should function. This information is written in a language that cells can understand. The alphabet for this language contains only four letters: A, G, C, and T. The letters stand for four chemicals contained in the DNA molecule: adenine (A), guanine (G), cytosine (C), and thymine (T).

8 HEREDITY

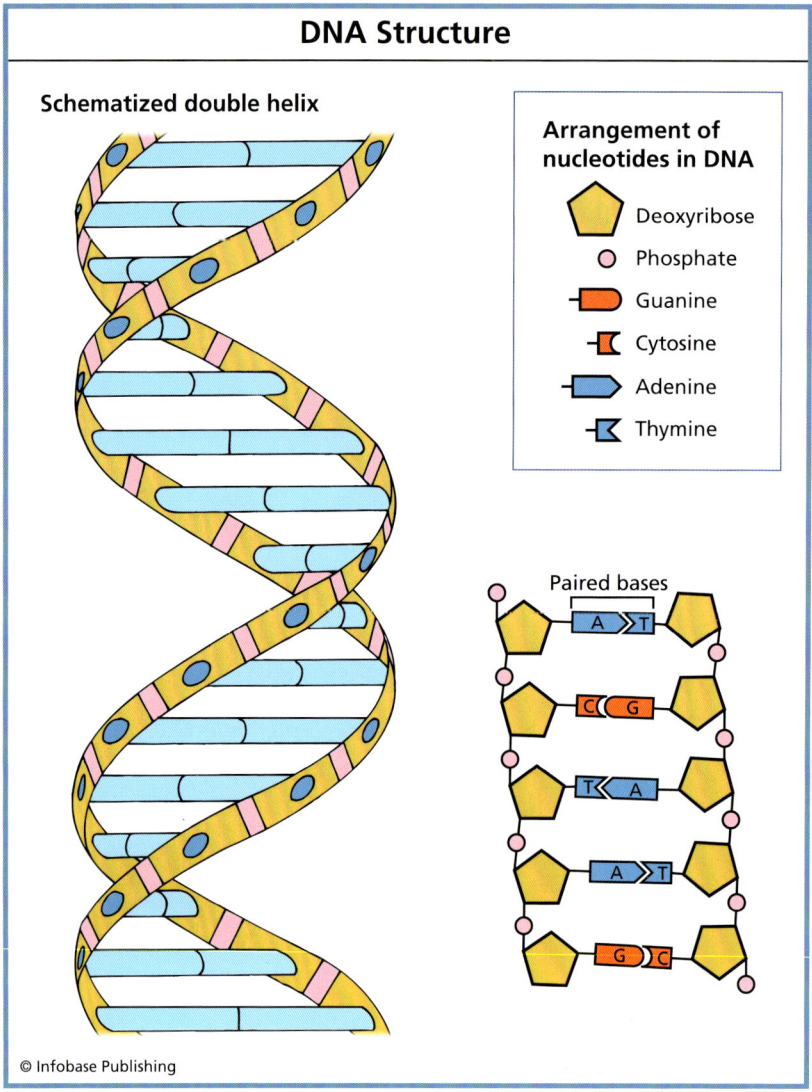

Figure 1.1 The structure of DNA looks a bit like a ladder. Its nucleotides are twisted in a double helix, joined together by base pairs of nucleotides. The base pairs make up the "rungs" of the ladder.

Human DNA contains approximately 6 billion of these letters, called nitrogen bases. The order of the bases in the DNA molecule determines an organism's traits, in the same way that different orders of letters make up different words and different sequences of words make up different sentences. More than 99% of this sequence is exactly the same in all humans. The differences in the DNA sequence are what make each human unique (Figure 1.1).

Junk DNA

Molecular biologists, scientists who study biology at the microscopic level, commonly call the DNA between genes "junk DNA." As far as scientists know, these portions of the DNA do not code for any particular protein. In the past, more than 95% of DNA was called junk because it had no known function. However, scientists are beginning to find that this so-called junk DNA might not be junk after all.

After studying the DNA code in several different types of animals, scientists were very surprised to find that these noncoding DNA sequences seem to be very well preserved from species to species. In other words, there are large chunks of DNA that are exactly the same in humans and in other species like mice and rats. It is not just one small sequence, either. Scientists found 480 sections of DNA that were exactly the same in humans, mice, and rats. In addition, the scientists only looked at sections that were at least 200 bases long. This means that the possibility of the sequences being exactly the same just by chance is quite small. These same regions were also close matches in chickens, dogs, and fish.

Scientists call these sections of the DNA "super-conserved" regions because they seem to have remained unchanged over the 400 million years of evolution that separate rodents, chickens, and fish from humans. It is possible that these regions are essential for survival. That would explain why they have not changed over time. Scientists now suspect that, rather than being junk, the noncoding DNA may somehow regulate, or control, how the coding DNA functions.

GENES

During reproduction, DNA is passed down from parent to child. Parts of the DNA molecule contain sequences of bases that tell the cell how and when to make **proteins**, and which proteins to make. Much of the work that needs to be done in order to keep the human body functioning correctly is carried out by proteins. The parts of the DNA sequence that contain the instructions on how and when to make a protein are called **genes** (Figure 1.2). Some genes carry a code to tell a cell how to make a particular protein. Other genes tell the cell when to make them.

In humans, genes can range in size from a few hundred to more than 2 million nitrogen bases. Scientists estimate that humans have between 20,000 and 25,000 genes in their **genomes**. A genome is the collection of all of the genes in an organism. All cells that contain DNA contain a complete genome, but some genes are switched "on" while others are switched "off" in certain cells. The genes that are active contain all the information the cell needs to make the specific proteins needed for that cell, organ, or tissue to survive and function the way it should.

Every person has two copies of most genes in their genome. One copy of the gene comes from their mother, and the other one comes from their father. The two copies of the genes are not exactly the same. They contain small changes in the sequence of DNA bases. These two different versions of the same gene are called **alleles**. The small differences in the alleles cause offspring to resemble their parents without looking exactly the same as either parent (Figure 1.3).

CHROMOSOMES

The DNA molecule is very long and thin. Almost all cells in the human body contain a piece of DNA that is approximately one meter long. A cell's nucleus, however, is usually only about six micrometers across. Trying to stuff this much thin, and breakable, genetic material into the cell's nucleus would be difficult. Instead, the DNA molecule

An Introduction to Heredity **11**

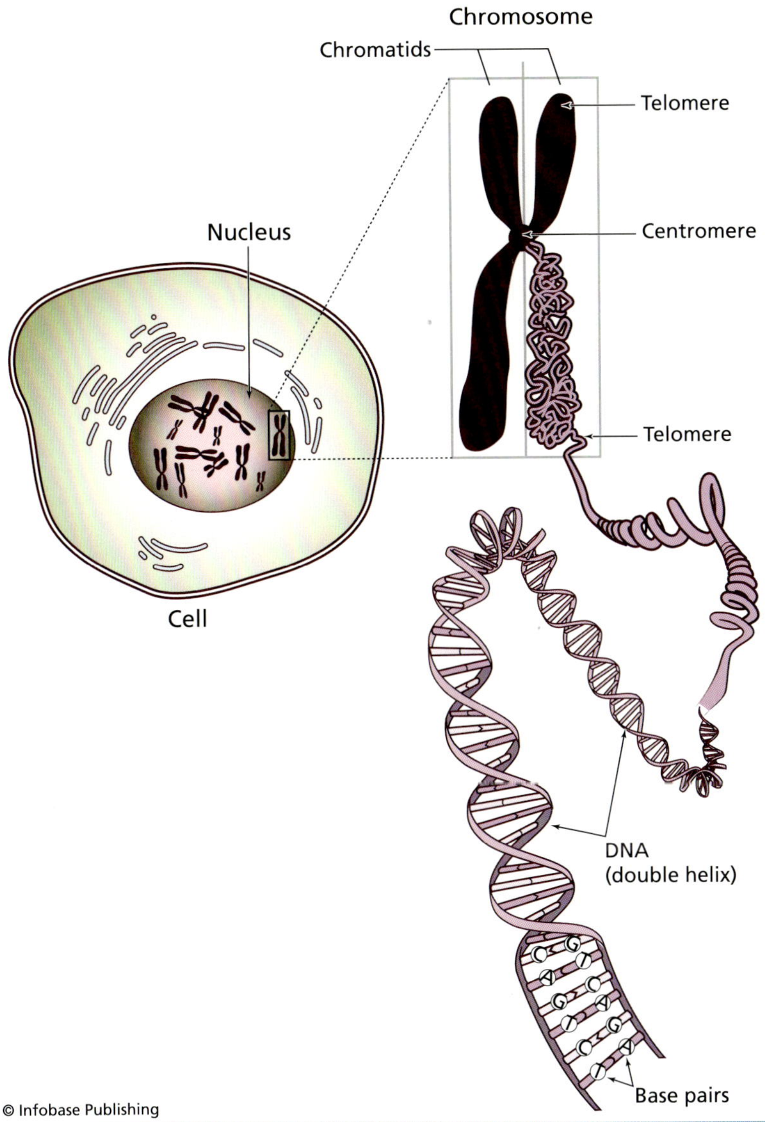

Figure 1.2 DNA is made up of sequences of genes. DNA molecules are wound around proteins called histones, and together they make up chromatin. Chromosomes are made up of chromatin, and can be found in the nucleus of a cell.

12 HEREDITY

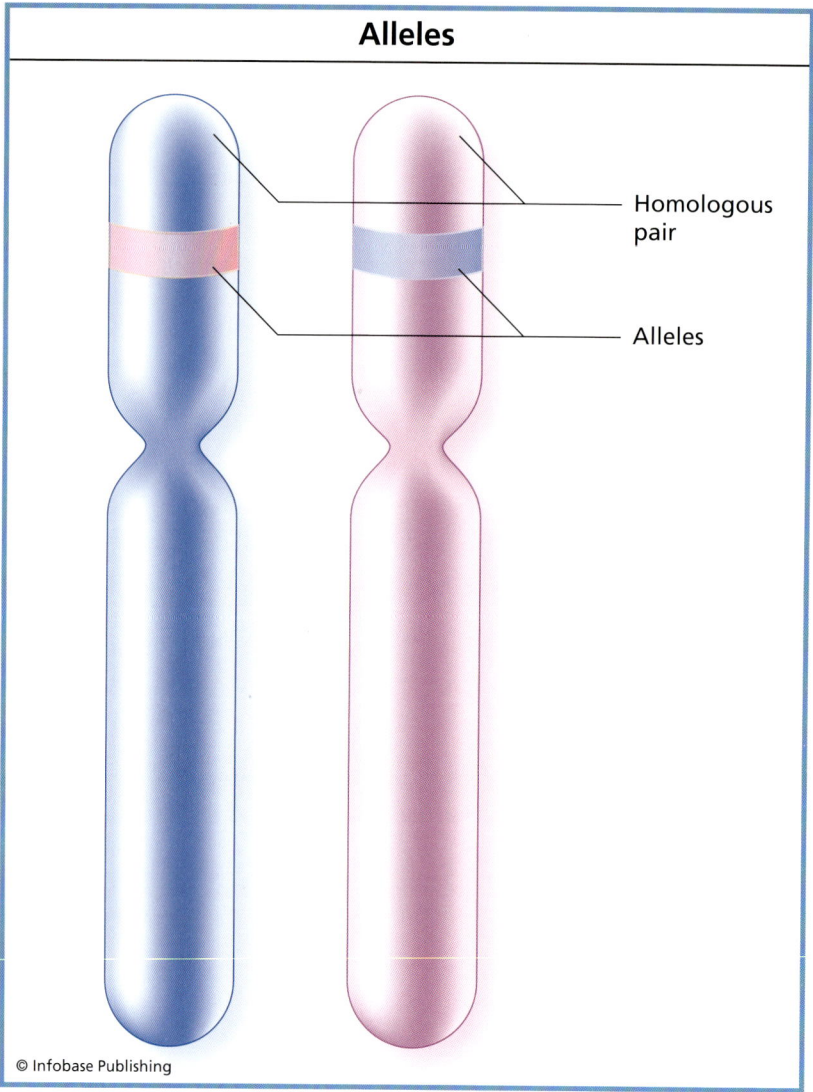

Figure 1.3 In an offspring, one chromosome comes from the offspring's father and the other comes from its mother. These paired chromosomes are called homologous chromosomes. On a homologous chromosome pair, there are two versions of every gene. These paired genes are called alleles.

and the genes it contains are wrapped around special proteins called **histones**, like a piece of string wrapped around a spool. The DNA molecule is too long to be wrapped around only one histone, though, so it is wrapped around several, making what looks like a string of beads. This string of beads is condensed into compact structures called **chromosomes**.

Chromosomes are made up of thousands of genes. Humans have 46 chromosomes, in 23 pairs. During a special type of cell division, called **meiosis**, the chromosome number from each parent is divided in half so there are 23 chromosomes in the mother's egg and 23 chromosomes in the father's sperm cells. When egg and sperm meet during fertilization, the 23 chromosomes from the mother and 23 chromosomes from the father combine, making 46 chromosomes for the resulting embryo. Because chromosomes come in pairs, so do genes. The two different copies of the genes are alleles.

RECESSIVE AND DOMINANT TRAITS

The alleles that are passed down from parent to child can be dominant, recessive, or a combination of the two. Dominant traits can mask (cover up) the appearance of a recessive trait in the offspring. In order for a **recessive genetic trait** to be expressed in the next generation, both parents must pass on the gene for that trait. A **dominant genetic trait**, on the other hand, will be expressed if either mom or dad, or both, pass on the allele for the trait.

Take the trait for dimples, for example. To have dimples is a dominant trait. To not have dimples is a recessive trait. On paper, geneticists show that a trait is dominant by using uppercase letters. They might use the letter "D" to represent dimples, for example. Recessive traits are indicated by lowercase letters (d). Therefore, if a child has no dimples, both parents must carry the no-dimple allele and pass those alleles on to the child. This makes the child **homozygous** for this trait because both alleles are the same (dd). But what if mom has dimples and dad does not? Will the child automatically have dimples? It depends. If dad does not have dimples, then he must be homozygous for the no-dimple trait because the no-dimples trait is recessive. It is possible that mom is homozygous for the dominant dimples trait. If this is the case, all of the couple's children will have dimples because mom's dominant allele will mask dad's allele and allow the trait to be expressed.

	d	d
D	Dd dimples	Dd dimples
D	Dd dimples	Dd dimples

There is another possibility, though. Mom could be **heterozygous** for the dimple trait. Heterozygous means that mom has two different alleles for the dimple trait—one dominant and one recessive (Dd). Mom can pass on either the dominant or the recessive gene to her child. If she passes on the dominant one (and dad passes on one of his recessive alleles), the child will have dimples and be heterozygous for the dimple trait. If she passes on the recessive allele to the child, the child will not have dimples and be homozygous for the recessive no-dimple trait.

	d	d
D	Dd dimples	Dd dimples
d	dd no dimples	dd no dimples

Which Traits Do You Have?

There are several other human genetic traits that follow the same simple, dominant-recessive pattern. Free earlobes, those that hang below the attachment point on the head, for example, are a dominant trait. Attached earlobes are recessive. Having straight thumbs is dominant over curved ones. On the other hand, having bent pinkies is dominant over straight pinkies. Being able to roll your tongue into a tube is a dominant trait. A widow's peak, or a V-shaped hairline, is dominant over a straight hairline. So which traits do you have? Can you determine which parent any of your traits come from? Do your parents carry the dominant or recessive allele for the traits, or do they carry both?

GENOTYPES AND PHENOTYPES

An organism's outward, physical appearance is called its **phenotype**. Dominant traits, such as dimples or a bent pinkie, for example, will show up in someone's phenotype. Recessive traits show up only if the person is homozygous for the recessive trait. Phenotype is determined by the person's DNA code, which makes up an organism's **genotype**.

Even if a person does not show a genetic trait, such as a curved thumb or a straight hairline, it does not mean that an allele for these traits does not exist in that person's genotype. If they are heterozygous for a recessive trait, the trait will be masked by a dominant allele and will not show up in their phenotype. However, they can still pass that allele down to the next generation, where it may or may not be expressed. This explains how recessive traits continue to be passed on. It also explains why some people are said to look more like a grandparent or a great aunt or uncle than they look like their parents.

Early Ideas about Heredity

People have always been interested in how a child comes to look like other members of its family. However, scientists did not discover DNA, genes, and chromosomes until relatively recently. But that did not stop people in earlier times from taking a guess about how heredity works. For the most part, their beliefs came from interpretations of what they saw. In other words, their conclusions were not tested using the scientific method; they were based only on untested observations.

Pythagoras (ca. 580–500 B.C.), a Greek philosopher and mathematician, for example, thought that all the necessary hereditary material came from the father, and that the mother only provided a place and food for the baby to grow. He also believed that this hereditary material was gathered from all over the father's body to pass on to his offspring.

However, Pythagoras's theory did not explain why a baby might have dad's nose but also have mom's hands. So Empedocles (ca. 490–430 B.C.), another Greek philosopher, explained this lapse in Pythagoras's theory by saying that both mom and dad possessed hereditary material that was passed on to their offspring through sexual fluid.

Building on the ideas of Pythagoras and Empedocles, Aristotle (384–322 B.C.) believed that while, in fact, both mother and father did contribute hereditary material to the unborn baby, it was not due to the sharing of sexual fluids, but to the sharing of blood. Aristotle believed that semen was a man's purified blood. When this purified blood commingled with the menstrual blood in a woman, the result was a child that shared traits with both mom and dad. Some scholars believe that Aristotle's thoughts are where the terms such as *blue blood* and *bloodline* come from when people speak of hereditary traits.

It took almost 2,000 years to shake off Aristotle's idea. William Harvey (1578–1657), an English physician who mainly studied the heart and circulatory system and explained how the beating of the human heart circulates blood throughout the body, also studied reproduction, primarily in chickens and deer. Through his research, Harvey came to understand that menstrual blood had nothing to do with the formation of a baby. Harvey thought that human babies were made much the same way chicks were, by the fusion of sperm and eggs. It turns out that Harvey was right, but it would take more than 200 years to prove it.

Twenty years after Harvey died, Dutch scientist Antonie van Leeuwenhoek (1632–1723) successfully invented a microscope that could reveal the sperm in semen. Leeuwenhoek's invention sparked the idea that all living things arise from interactions between cells. This idea helped to dispel a popular notion that had been around since the time of Aristotle—the theory of spontaneous generation. People, including scientists, believed spontaneous generation could occur, or that living things could arise spontaneously from inanimate objects.

SPONTANEOUS GENERATION

People who believed in spontaneous generation thought, for example, that flies could arise from a piece of meat. They believed this because they observed that meat left on a kitchen counter was quickly swarmed with flies. Therefore, they believed that the flies must have been spontaneously born from the meat. There was other "proof," too. Every year, the Nile River flooded. Along with the floodwaters, the overflowing river brought fertile soil and frogs to the land. These frogs did not exist when the land was drier. This gave people the idea that frogs must come from mud. Another observation that led people to believe that the theory of spontaneous generation was true was the number of mice in barns that contained moldy grain. Because mice were almost always found where there was moldy grain, people believed that the mice actually came from the moldy grain.

Although Leeuwenhoek's microscope helped put this idea of spontaneous generation to rest, it was the experiments of an Italian physician named Francesco Redi (1626–1697) that truly disproved the idea. In 1668, Redi set up an experiment by putting pieces of meat into several wide-mouth jars. Redi's hypothesis stated that if flies came from meat, all of the jars in the experiment should have maggots (fly larvae) and flies in them by the end of the experiment. For his control group, Redi allowed several of the jars with meat in them to stay open to the air. These jars simulated the conditions meat would encounter in a butcher shop of that time period. For his experimental groups, he prepared several other jars that contained meat and divided them into two groups. Redi covered the mouths of the jars in one group with gauze and the other group with lids. Then he waited. Each day, he counted and recorded the number of maggots or flies around each jar in each group.

Redi observed flies in and around the jars that were left open to the air. Soon maggots appeared on the meat in those jars, and then there were more flies than ever. While Redi never observed flies inside the jars covered with gauze, he did see flies sitting on the gauze at the mouth of the jars. Eventually some maggots were seen inside these jars. No flies or maggots were ever observed in the jars sealed with a lid.

Redi concluded that in the jars open to the air, flies entered the jars and laid eggs on the meat, and then the eggs hatched and the maggots emerged. These maggots eventually turned into adult flies. Even though flies could not enter the jars covered with gauze, they could lay eggs on the gauze. Redi also deduced that either the eggs fell through the gauze onto the meat and then hatched, or the eggs hatched on the gauze and the maggots fell through and onto the meat. Either way, the eggs and then the maggots came from flies that were on the outside of the jar. Because there were no flies inside the jars sealed with a lid, they could not lay eggs and there were

Early Ideas about Heredity   **19**

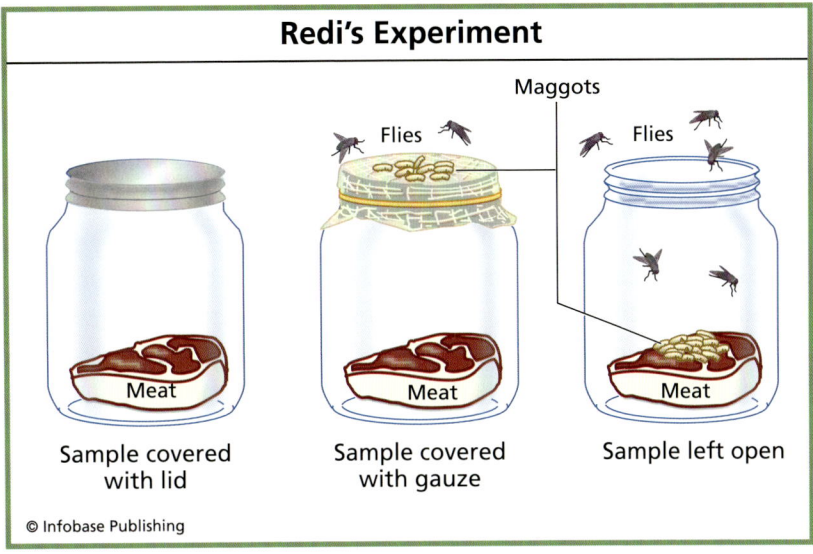

Figure 2.1 Redi's experiment disproved spontaneous generation, using three different jars to show that flies could not spontaneously arise from meat. The jar with the lid prevented flies from laying their eggs on the meat, and so no maggots (which would turn into flies) appeared. The open jar and the jar with gauze allowed for eggs to be laid onto the meat or on the gauze, respectively.

no maggots. From these observations, Redi concluded that flies do not arise from meat—only flies can make other flies (Figure 2.1).

One would think that this would have been the end of the spontaneous generation debate, but it was not. People were willing to believe that larger organisms, such as flies and humans, could not be produced by spontaneous generation and, in fact, needed parents. But with the better microscopes of the 1600s, people were seeing all sorts of bacteria, yeast, and other single-celled organisms. They did not know where these tiny organisms came from, but they always seemed to be present in spoiled broth. So it seemed logical to people at the time that these microorganisms spontaneously generated in spoiled broth.

In 1745, a Scottish clergyman and naturalist named John Needham (1713–1781) claimed that all inorganic molecules, such as air and the oxygen in it, contained a "life force" that allowed spontaneous generation to occur. Needham proved his claim by boiling some broth (to kill any microorganisms already present in the broth), pouring it into "clean" flasks, and capping the flasks with natural cork stoppers. When microorganisms still grew in the broth, Needham was convinced that his conclusions about a "life force" were correct.

Not everyone was convinced, however. A few years later, Lazzaro Spallanzani (1729–1799), an Italian biologist, tried Needham's experiments again. Spallanzani boiled some broth for an hour. Then he took some of the boiled broth and sealed it in several glass flasks by melting the mouths of the flasks shut. Other portions of broth were put into flasks capped with natural cork stoppers, just like in Needham's experiment. For his last experimental group, Spallanzani boiled broth for only a few minutes, put it into flasks, and melted the mouths of the flasks shut.

Spallanzani found that the only flasks that did not contain microorganisms were the flasks containing broth that had been boiled for an hour and then sealed by melting the mouths of the flasks shut. From these results, Spallanzani was convinced that microorganisms could not be spontaneously generated, either.

Needham, however, was not convinced. He believed that the microorganisms could not be spontaneously generated in Spallanzani's sealed flasks because the "life force" was destroyed during the extensive boiling time, and that it could not enter the flask after it had been sealed. This created such a big argument between the two scientists that the Paris Academy of Sciences offered a prize to the first person who could develop and carry out an experiment to put the argument to rest.

In 1859, Louis Pasteur (1822–1895) claimed the prize. In his experiment, Pasteur also boiled broth to kill all of the bacteria in it. But he boiled the broth in different-shaped flasks. He then allowed the flasks, containing the sterilized broth, to cool. The flasks in the control group had straight necks, open to the outside air and any bacteria in it. Other flasks had thin, S-shaped necks, called swan-neck flasks; they would allow air and, therefore, the "life force" that Needham insisted needed to be present, to enter the flasks—but bacteria would settle out, due to gravity, on the necks of the flasks and not reach the broth. Pasteur found that broth in the straight-necked flasks spoiled, while broth in the swan-necked flasks did not, even though fresh air

Early Ideas about Heredity   21

could get into the flasks. This finally put to rest the idea of spontaneous generation.

PREFORMATION

Preformation was another idea that many intellectuals held during the seventeenth and eighteenth centuries. Preformationists believed that humans grew from tiny, fully formed humans that already existed in either the egg or the sperm. The miniature human was called a homunculus (Figure 2.2).

Dutch scientist Jan Swammerdam (1637–1680) believed that the miniature human was encapsulated in a man's sperm and that the mother was only a vessel for development of the fetus. But then, a century later, Swiss scientist Charles Bonnet (1720–1793) said, no, the miniature human was actually in the mother's egg.

In 1745, however, French mathematician and biologist Pierre-Louis Moreau de Maupertuis (1698–1759) argued that preformation would not explain the existence of babies born with birth defects. Instead, Maupertuis proposed that both parents had "particles" within their hereditary material that, when commingled, formed a baby. Maupertuis also believed that sometimes one parent's "particles" had a stronger influence over the development of the baby than the other parent's "particles." This was the precursor to the modern idea of dominant and recessive genes.

PANGENESIS THEORY

Charles Darwin (1809–1882), an English naturalist, is probably best known for his ideas about evolution and natural selection. Darwin's theory of natural selection states that those individuals in a population who carry the most advantageous traits will have a better chance at survival and reproduction. Therefore, these advantageous traits are passed on to offspring generation after generation. In this way, these traits are increased in the population.

Darwin believed that every organ and tissue in the body produced small particles, which he called "gemmules," that flowed

230   ESSAY DE DIOPTRIQUE.
que la tête feroit peut-être plus grande à proportion du reste du corps, qu'on ne l'a deffinée icy.

Au reste, l'œuf n'eſt à proprement parler que ce qu'on appelle *placenta*, dont l'enfant, aprés y avoir demeuré un certain temps tout courbé & comme en peloton, brife en s'étendant & en s'allongeant le plus qu'il peut, les membranes qui le couvroient, & pofant fes pieds contre le *placenta*, qui refte attaché au fond de la matrice, fe pouffe ainfi avec la tête hors de fa prifon ; en quoi il eſt aidé par la mere, qui agitée par la douleur qu'elle en fent, pouffe le fond de la matrice en bas, & donne par confequent d'autant plus d'occafion à cet enfant de fe pouffer dehors & de venir ainfi au monde.

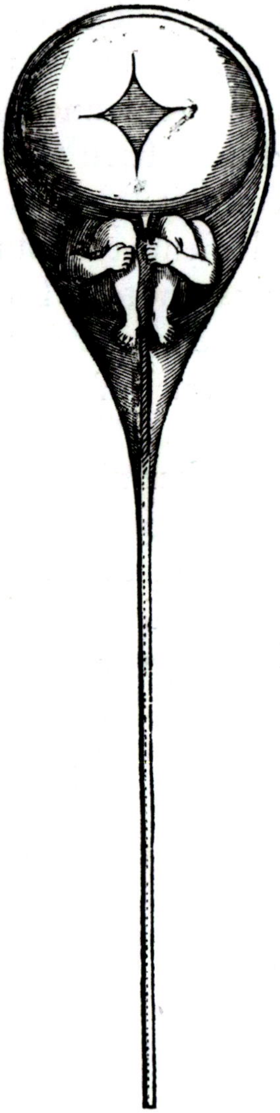

L'experience nous apprend que beaucoup d'animaux fortent à peu prés de cette maniere des œufs qui les renferment.

L'on peut pouffer bien plus loin cette nouvelle penfée de la generation, & dire que chacun de ces animaux

Figure 2.2 It was once believed that miniature, fully formed humans existed within the egg or the sperm—a concept known as preformation.

Early Ideas about Heredity

Selective Breeding

Just because scientists did not know exactly how heredity and genetics worked did not stop people from using what they observed. People have been manipulating the phenotypes of plants and animals for centuries. This practice is called selective breeding.

Farmers, for example, might selectively breed plants that are more resistant to disease or that yield a larger crop. Dairy farmers might selectively breed dairy cows that routinely produce more milk. Poultry farmers might selectively breed hens that lay the most eggs.

If a dairy farmer crosses a cow that produces a lot of milk with a bull that comes from a line of long-lived cattle, the resulting offspring could carry both of these advantageous traits. The offspring is called a hybrid. Animal and plant hybrids are produced by crossing parents that are genetically different.

If this selective breeding goes on from generation to generation, there is a danger of losing genetic diversity. Genetic diversity is important because it allows organisms to adapt to adverse conditions such as a lack of food or outbreaks of disease. When animals or plants that have a desired trait are bred with another that has the same trait, other genes (the ones that do not code for the advantageous trait being selected for, but may code for other important traits) are in danger of getting permanently lost. This is called in-breeding depression. For this reason, breeders try very carefully to produce animals and plants that are heterozygous, in order to preserve genetic diversity.

through the body's bloodstream. He explained that these gemmules, which converged into sperm and egg that merged during fertilization, and "pangenes," which made up the hereditary material, were passed down to the offspring. This theory was called the pangenesis theory. Early on, Darwin also believed that a parent's pangenes could change throughout their lifetime. This would mean that offspring could receive traits that had changed during the parent's lifetime. Darwin later abandoned this part of his theory.

Gregor Mendel: The Father of Modern Genetics

Gregor Mendel (1822–1884) is often called the "father of heredity." Mendel was a monk and a high school physics, mathematics, and Greek teacher, but he was also one of the first genetics researchers. Most of Mendel's research was carried out in the Czechoslovakian monastery where he lived. He experimented with the way traits are passed from generation to generation in pea plants by researching seven main characteristics: flower color, flower position, stem length, pod shape, pod color, seed shape, and seed color (Figure 3.1).

Mendel picked the common pea plant, *Pisum sativum*, for his research because it is easy to grow in large numbers and its reproduction is easy to control. Pea plants have both stamens (the male reproductive organ in plants) and a pistil (the female reproductive organ). Under normal circumstances, these plants can self-pollinate, but they can also be cross-pollinated with other pea plants. Mendel allowed the plants to self-pollinate for several generations. During this time, he controlled access to other pea plants by covering the plants so pollen could not be transferred from one plant to another. In this way, Mendel was certain of the parentage of each plant. Eventually, he produced a plant that was purebred for whichever trait he was considering in his experiments at the time. The purebreds had

Gregor Mendel: The Father of Modern Genetics

Traits of Mendel's Pea Plants

Character	Dominant trait		Recessive trait	F₂ Generation Dominant:Recessive	Ratio
Flower color	 Purple	X	 White	705:224	3.15:1
Flower position	 Axial	X	 Terminal	651:207	3.14:1
Seed color	 Yellow	X	 Green	6022:2001	3.01:1
Seed shape	 Round	X	 Wrinkled	5474:1850	2.96:1
Pod shape	 Inflated	X	 Constricted	882:299	2.95:1
Pod color	 Green	X	 Yellow	428:152	2.82:1
Stem length	 Tall	X	 Dwarf	787:277	2.84:1

© Infobase Publishing

Figure 3.1 Gregor Mendel focused on seven main characteristics during his study of how traits are passed down from generation to generation in pea plants.

two identical alleles for that particular trait, meaning that they were homozygous. For example, one of the traits that interested Mendel was the pea plant's seed shape. The pea plant seeds (peas) came in two shapes, round or wrinkled. Therefore, he created purebred plants with round seeds (RR) and purebred plants with wrinkled seeds (rr).

Once he had purebreds for each trait, Mendel was ready to start his experiments. This time, he planned to crossbreed the purebreds. To do this, Mendel eliminated the possibility of self-pollination by carefully removing a plant's stamens before they were mature enough to pollinate the plant. Then, using a paint brush to apply pollen from a selected plant onto another plant, he was able to control the cross-pollination. Once again, this allowed Mendel to pinpoint the exact parentage of each pea plant.

To continue his study into the pea plants' seed shape, he painted pollen from a plant that had wrinkled peas (rr) onto a plant that had round peas (RR). He also did the reverse, painting pollen from a plant with round seeds onto a plant that had wrinkled seeds. Mendel found out that it did not matter which plant the pollen came from—the offspring were identical. However, it was possible that the origin of the pollen could have made a difference. By trying the experiment twice, using the pollen from one parent plant in one trial and the pollen from the other parent in the second, Mendel was following the proper scientific method.

The plants being cross-pollinated are called the parental generation, or the P generation. The offspring of this mating is called the first filial generation. Scientists abbreviate the first filial generation as F_1. Mendel discovered that the F_1 plants that resulted from a cross of a purebred parent plant with round peas, as well as one that had wrinkled peas, all had round seeds.

	r	r
R	Rr round peas	Rr round peas
R	Rr round peas	Rr round peas

Gregor Mendel: The Father of Modern Genetics

This observation led Mendel to define the trait that he could observe, in this case round peas, as the dominant trait. Mendel then allowed the plants in the F_1 generation to self-pollinate and produce an F_2, or second filial generation. To his surprise, some of the plants in the F_2 generation had wrinkled seeds. The wrinkled pea trait had reappeared.

	R	r
R	RR round peas	Rr round peas
r	Rr round peas	rr wrinkled peas

Mendel conducted enough experiments to convince himself that this did, indeed, happen every time he crossed plants with round seeds with those that had wrinkled seeds. He also figured out that every time he did that same cross, 25% of the offspring in the F_2 generation had wrinkled seeds. Mendel decided to call the trait that disappeared in the F_1 generation and then reappeared in the F_2 generation the recessive trait.

Again, Mendel allowed the F_2 plants to self-pollinate. He discovered that the F_2 plants that had wrinkled seeds produced only plants with wrinkled seeds. One-third of the round-seeded plants also produced only round-seeded plants when they self-pollinated. The other two-thirds of the round-seeded plants produced both round-seeded and wrinkled-seeded plants in the same ratio that the F_1 generation produced.

PUNNETT SQUARES

Many years after Mendel's experiments, an English geneticist named Reginald Punnett (1875–1967) developed a way to visualize genetic crosses like the ones done by Mendel. The diagram is called a Punnett square, and it helps biologists determine the probability that an offspring of a genetic cross will inherit a particular trait.

In Mendel's original experiment with round versus wrinkled pea plants, he crossed plants that always produced round seeds with those that always produced wrinkled seeds. These plants were homozygous for either round or wrinkled seeds. Mendel found out that round seeds was the dominant trait (because when he crossed round-seeded plants with wrinkled-seeded plants he always got round-seeded plants). To show that a trait is dominant in a Punnett square, geneticists use an uppercase letter. Recessive traits are often given the same letter, but it is lowercase. So, for example, round seeds would be designated by an "R," while wrinkled peas would be designated with an "r." Remember that each plant would have two alleles for each trait—one from each parent (even if it self-pollinated, it would get one allele from the male part of the plant and one allele from the female part). If the plant is homozygous for the dominant round peas, both alleles would carry the "R" designation. If the plant is homozygous for the recessive wrinkled peas, both alleles would be "r."

A cross where only one trait is being considered is called a **monohybrid cross**. A Punnett square for a monohybrid cross has four boxes like the one shown below.

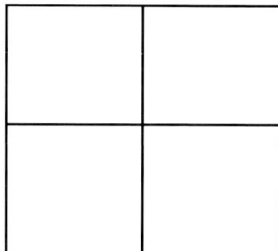

The alleles for one parent are written on the side of the Punnett square, while the other parent's alleles are written across the top (which parent goes on top and which one goes on the side is unimportant).

Gregor Mendel: The Father of Modern Genetics 29

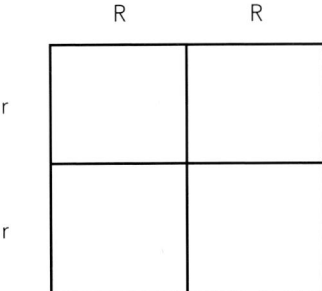

To find out the possible genotypes of the offspring, bring down the "R" that belongs to the round-seeded parent from the top of the Punnett square, and bring the "r" that belongs to the wrinkled-seeded parent from the left, and place them into the upper left-hand corner box. By convention, geneticists write the capital letter first.

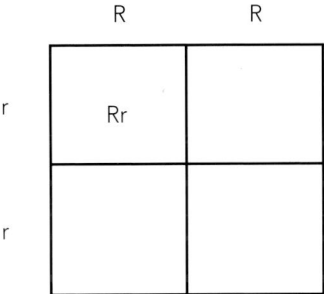

Now do the same thing for the remaining boxes.

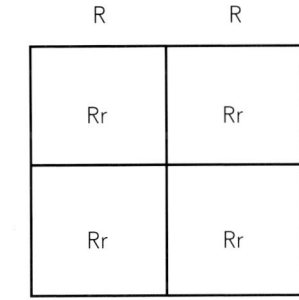

30 HEREDITY

As the Punnett square shows, when a homozygous round-seeded plant is crossed with a homozygous wrinkled-seeded plant, the genotype of the offspring will always be "Rr." Because the alleles are different (one is "R" while the other is "r"), the offspring will be heterozygous. And because the allele for round seeds is dominant, the offspring will have round seeds. This represents Mendel's F_1 experimental data.

Now try the same thing for the F_2 generation. Remember that in this generation, Mendel allowed the F_1 offspring to self-pollinate. Because all of the offspring have a genotype of "Rr," Mendel was crossing two "Rr" plants (even if he did not know that at the time). Because these plants are heterozygous, they make two different types of **gametes** (eggs and sperm, or pollen). One type of gamete contains the allele for round seeds (R) and the other one contains the allele for wrinkled seeds (r). The set-up for the Punnett square would look like this:

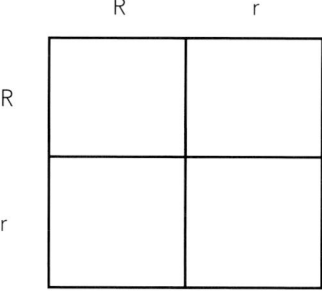

Fill in the Punnett square like the one above by bringing down the allele belonging to one parent from the top and bringing the other allele over from the left to fill in the boxes.

	R	r
R	RR	Rr
r	Rr	rr

As this Punnett square shows, an offspring produced by crossing two heterozygous plants can have three possible genotypes: RR, Rr, or rr. Because round seeds are dominant, these three genotypes can result in two different phenotypes: round peas (RR or Rr) or wrinkled peas (rr). This Punnett square can help explain Mendel's results from his F_2 crosses. It shows the probability (chance) of an offspring possessing a particular genotype. There is a one in four, or 25%, chance that an offspring of this cross will have the genotype "RR." There is a 50% chance that the offspring will have the genotype "Rr." And there is a 25% chance that the offspring will be homozygous for the wrinkled-seeded trait (their genotype is "rr") and show wrinkled seeds.

Therefore, when Mendel allowed the wrinkled-seeded plants (rr) to self-pollinate, only plants with wrinkled seeds would be the result.

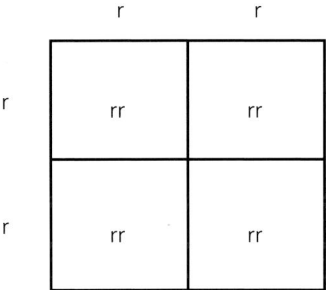

Of the plants that exhibited the round-seeded phenotype, one-third has the genotype "RR." If these plants are allowed to self-pollinate, all of their offspring will be homozygous for the dominant round-seeded trait.

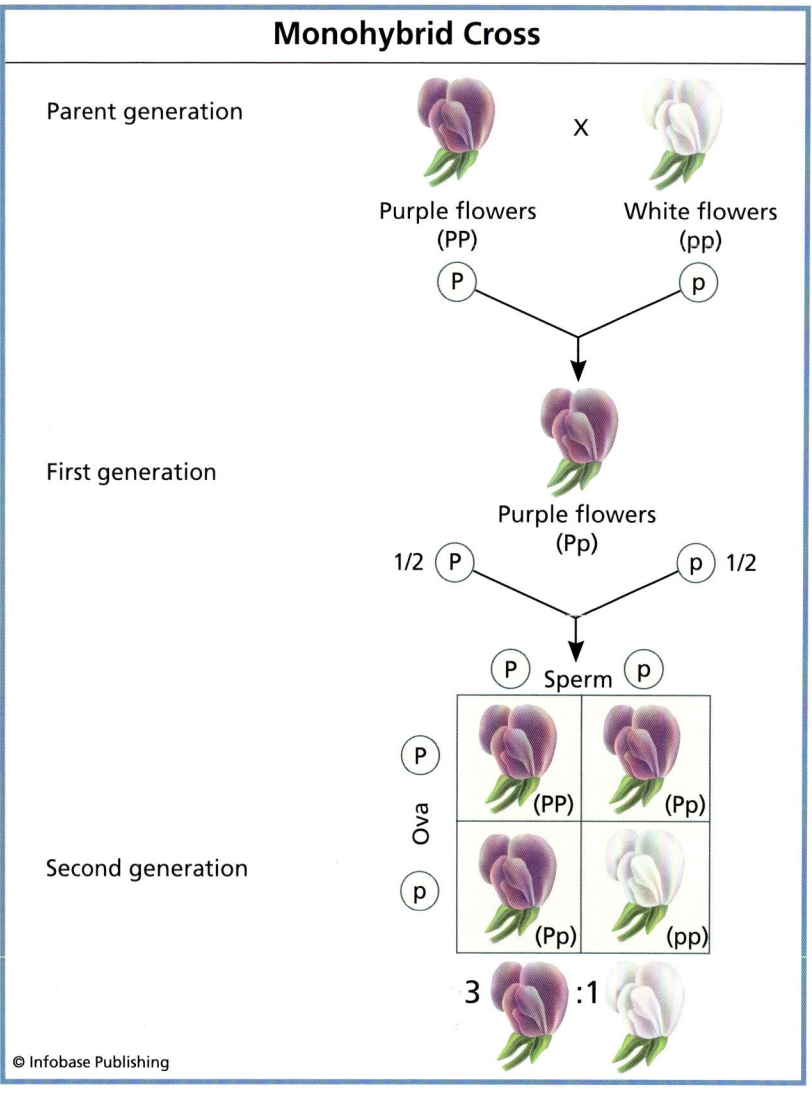

Figure 3.2 In one of his experiments, Mendel cross-pollinated two true-breeding flowers, one purple and one white. The first generation's offspring all displayed purple petals, but the second generation produced some purple flowers, and some white. This led Mendel to conclude that some traits, like the purple flower, are dominant, and some, like the white flower, are recessive.

The other two-thirds of the round-seeded plants have the heterogeneous genotype "Rr," just like the F_1 generation crossed in this example. Just like the F_1 generation, when these plants self-pollinate, they will produce both round-seeded and wrinkled-seeded plants in the same ratio that the F_1 generation produced them in.

MENDEL'S RESULTS

It took Mendel seven years to cross, observe, and record the results of thousands of plants in order to prove his ideas of how traits were passed from one generation to another. His research helped him disprove the idea of "blending," which was popular at the time. The blending theory stated that the parents' traits were "blended" to give the offspring an average of their traits. In other words, if one parent is tall and one is short, proponents of the blending theory would expect all the offspring of these parents to be medium height.

Through his research, however, Mendel was able to show that a cross between a tall pea plant (TT or Tt) and a dwarf pea plant (tt) would produce generations of plants that are either tall or dwarf. But none of the plants produced by any of these crosses were medium-tall and, therefore, were not blended.

	T	t
t	Tt	tt
t	Tt	tt

The Punnett square shows that the ratio of offspring in a cross between a heterozygous tall plant (Tt) and a homozygous dwarf plant (tt) is 50% tall (Tt and Tt) and 50% dwarf (tt and tt).

A cross between a homozygous tall plant (TT) and a dwarf plant (tt) would lead to all tall plants with a heterozygous genotype (Tt).

	T	T
t	Tt	Tt
t	Tt	Tt

But there are still no medium-sized plants—only tall and dwarf. Mendel hypothesized that rather than blending, alleles (which he called "units" or "factors") are randomly selected to be passed on to the next generation. This hypothesis is now called Mendel's first law, or the law of segregation.

From his research, Mendel concluded that physical traits were passed from parent to offspring through units or factors that are now called alleles. He also determined that each parent had two factors per trait. After studying the results of his experiments, Mendel observed some patterns. From these patterns, Mendel developed his basic rules of heredity:

- Traits are inherited independently of other traits.
- Some alleles are dominant, while others are recessive.
- An offspring inherits half of its alleles from each parent.
- Different offspring of the same parents get different combinations of alleles.

INDEPENDENT ASSORTMENT

Punnett squares can also be used to predict the inheritance ratio of offspring that contain two different traits at the same time. This type of cross is called a **dihybrid cross**. Take the flowers of the pea plant, for example. Mendel discovered that purple flowers (P) are dominant over white flowers (p) and axial flowers (A), which grow in the middle of a stem, are dominant over terminal flowers (a), which grow at the end of the stem (Figure 3.2). If Mendel crossed a pea plant that was homozygous for white terminal flowers with a pea plant that was homozygous for purple axial flowers, what would the Punnett square look like?

The genotype for the plant that is homozygous for white terminal flowers must be "ppaa," and the genotype for the plant that is homozygous for purple axial flowers would have to be "PPAA." The plant that produces white terminal flowers can make gametes that contain only the alleles "p" and "a," while the one that produces the purple axial flowers can make only gametes that contain the alleles "P" and "A."

	PA	PA
pa	PpAa	PpAa
pa	PpAa	PpAa

As the Punnett square for this parent generation shows, all of the offspring of this cross would appear to have purple, axial flowers. But all of the offspring also carry the recessive white, terminal flower alleles that cannot be seen in this F_1 generation. The entire F_1 generation is heterozygous for the color and the flower position alleles. If the F_1 generation is allowed to self-pollinate, then things get interesting. During Mendel's experiments, he determined that two different traits were always inherited independently of one another. This idea is called Mendel's second law, or the law of independent assortment. In this case, each plant can produce four different gametes—PA, Pa, pA, and pa. These are all of the possible combinations of the two alleles.

	PA	Pa	pA	pa
PA	PPAA	PPAa	PpAA	PpAa
Pa	PPAa	PPaa	PpAa	Ppaa
pA	PpAA	PpAa	ppAA	ppAa
pa	PpAa	Ppaa	ppAa	ppaa

Rediscovery of Mendel's Work

Mendel's research was published in 1866, but was largely ignored at the time. Then, in 1868, he was promoted to abbot of the monastery where he worked. Consumed with church business, Mendel dropped his scientific pursuits. He died of a chronic kidney disease in 1884.

Thirty-four years after the publication of Mendel's results and 16 years after his death, his research was rediscovered independently by Hugo de Vries of the Netherlands, Erich von Tschermak of Austria, and Carl Correns of Germany. Each of these men was working on different hybrid plants and determined their own laws of how traits are inherited from generation to generation. Before publishing their results, however, each man searched through the scientific literature, which is a part of the scientific publishing process. During this process, de Vries, von Tschermak, and Correns all came across Mendel's 1866 publication stating his laws of inheritance. When each of the three men published the results of their experiments, they re-announced Mendel's work to the scientific world and described how their work confirmed Mendel's results.

The Punnett square shows the following: 9 of the 16 offspring of these F_2 plants will have purple, axial flowers (genotypes: PPAA, PPAa, PpAA, PpAa); 3 offspring will have purple, terminal flowers (genotypes: PPaa and Ppaa); 3 offspring will have white, axial flowers (genotypes: ppAA and ppAa); and 1 offspring will have white, terminal flowers (genotype: ppaa). Mendel realized that this ratio, 9:3:3:1, happened every time he crossed plants that were heterozygous for two independently assorting traits.

Chromosome Theory of Heredity

In the early 1900s, Thomas Hunt Morgan (1866–1945), a biologist who studied fruit flies, was about to make his contribution to the science of genetics. The scientific name for the common fruit fly is *Drosophila melanogaster* (*D. melanogaster*). Morgan found that when he crossed a red-eyed female fly with a white-eyed male fly, all of their offspring had red eyes. But when he took some of these red-eyed offspring and crossed them with their siblings, the white-eyed trait reappeared in the offspring. Morgan noticed that all of these white-eyed F_2 generation flies had something in common—they were all male. From the results of his experiments, Morgan determined that eye color in the fruit fly is linked specifically to the X chromosome (Figure 4.1). Morgan also proposed the idea that genes are lined up, one after another, on a chromosome. His work firmly established the idea that traits are inherited via chromosomes. In 1933, Morgan was awarded the Nobel Prize in Physiology or Medicine for his discovery of how chromosomes are involved in heredity.

In 1913, a student of Morgan's named Alfred Sturtevant (1891–1970) created a genetic map of the *D. melanogaster* genome. This was the world's first genetic map. Sturtevant published the map for his Ph.D. thesis.

Chromosome Theory of Heredity 39

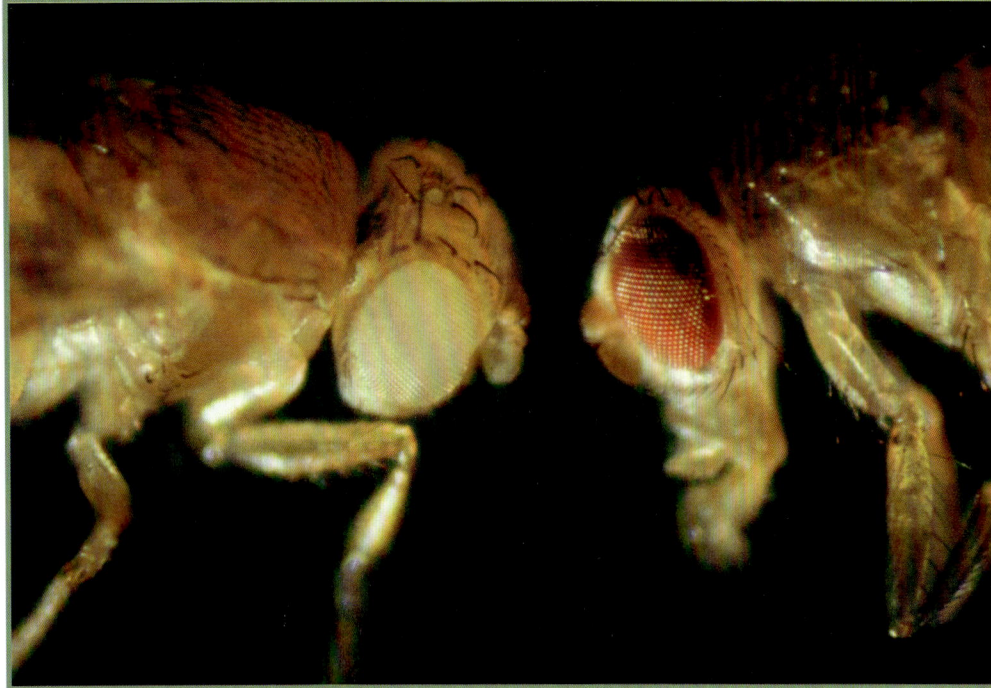

Figure 4.1 Thomas Hunt Morgan studied fruit flies—which are easy to breed in large numbers and have therefore been used for years in genetic studies—and learned that eye color is linked to the X chromosome in fruit flies.

GENETIC MUTATIONS AND RADIATION

Alfred Sturtevant was not the only student of Morgan's who was studying *D. melanogaster*. Hermann Joseph Muller (1890–1967) also studied in Morgan's laboratory. But Muller got tired of waiting for the fruit flies to mutate on their own. In 1927, Muller tried to use heat to increase the rate of mutation. However, he was unsatisfied with the number of mutations that resulted. So he exposed the flies to X-ray radiation. In that experiment, Muller not only got the mutations he was looking for, but he also proved that exposure to radiation could change genetic material.

After these experiments, Muller became a vocal advocate for limiting unnecessary exposure to radiation. He warned about

The Fruit Fly and Genetic Research

By the end of the 1980s, scientists had found over 3,000 mutations in fruit flies. Along with the white-eyed mutants that Morgan discovered, mutant flies turned up with pink, purple, maroon, and bright-red eyes, rather than the normal brick-red color. By manipulating a fly's genetic structure, scientists were able to produce flies with a double set of wings, miniature wings, or no wings at all. They made hairy flies and bald flies. They also produced flies that had functioning eyes on their wings, abdomen, legs, or even on the tips of their antennae. But why do this? What is the benefit?

The study of fruit flies has proven beneficial because, perhaps surprisingly, fruit flies and humans have a lot in common. In fact, about 50% of the genes that code for proteins in *D. melanogaster* are also found in mammals. In addition, scientists have found stretches of DNA code in the fruit fly that match the DNA code of 61% of human genes known to cause disease. Currently, *D. melanogaster*

---

radiation's link to increased genetic mutations and cancer. In 1946, Muller was awarded the Nobel Prize in Physiology or Medicine for his discovery that X-rays produce genetic mutations.

JUMPING GENES

The first American woman to win an unshared Nobel Prize was Barbara McClintock (1902–1992), an American geneticist who was recognized for her discovery of "jumping genes." McClintock did her experiments on maize, or corn, in the mid-1940s. She was studying the color variations on a single cob of corn and found that two genes, called "controlling genes," determined the color of each kernel. However, these controlling genes did not always show up in the same place on the corn's chromosomes, and kernel color also depended on is being used to model human diseases, such as Parkinson's disease and Huntington's disease.

Studying model organisms, such as fruit flies or mice, allows researchers to manipulate genetic factors and determine what will happen. Scientists could not, for example, arrange to cross two humans to see how their children turned out. Nor could they purposely disable a gene in a human. Studying complex model organisms, however, can tell the scientists what is likely to happen in humans without actually experimenting on them.

D. melanogaster is a good model organism for genetic research because the flies reproduce quickly, and many generations can be studied in a short period of time. The average lifespan of an adult fruit fly is only a couple of weeks, but in those weeks, a pair of flies can produce hundreds of offspring. These offspring become sexually mature in a week and can begin the cycle again. Fruit flies are also tiny (about 3–5 millimeters [mm] long and 2 mm wide), so they do not take up much laboratory space. They are easy to feed, and male fruit flies can be distinguished from female fruit flies just by looking at them.

where these controlling genes ended up on the chromosome. Transposable genes, or transposons, are sequences of DNA that can move from one region of a chromosome to another. They can even move to a different chromosome entirely. Because of their mobility, transposable genes have also become known as "jumping genes" (Figure 4.2).

Although McClintock discovered jumping genes in the 1940s, her research was largely ignored for several decades because her ideas about moving genes did not agree with anything known about genes at the time. Finally, in the 1970s and early 1980s, better scientific techniques were discovered that allowed other scientists to confirm McClintock's findings. In 1983, McClintock was awarded the Nobel Prize for Physiology or Medicine for her discovery of transposons.

Because transposons can disrupt normal gene function if they land in the wrong place on a chromosome, scientists today suspect

42 HEREDITY

Figure 4.2 Transposable genes, also known as jumping genes, can move to different parts of the chromosomes or to different chromosomes entirely. Barbara McClintock discovered these genes while studying maize, learning that kernel color depended on the location of two "controlling genes"—which determine kernel color—on the chromosome.

that transposons may be responsible for some genetic diseases such as hemophilia, leukemia, and breast cancer.

DISCOVERING THE STRUCTURE OF DNA

Scientists in the 1830s and early 1840s knew that chromosomes were passed from one generation to the next, but they did not know what chromosomes were made of. This mystery started to unravel in 1869, when Johann Friedrich Miescher (1844–1895), a Swiss biochemist, was doing experiments on white blood cells that he obtained from the pus-filled bandages of wounded soldiers in a local hospital. During these experiments, Miescher added some chemicals to the white blood cells, which resulted in the formation of a white precipitate (a solid that is separated from a solution or suspension by a chemical or physical change). This precipitate was a new substance, and Miescher believed, correctly, that this new chemical came from the nuclei of the white blood cells. He named the new chemical *nuclein*.

Miescher went on to show that nuclein could be isolated not just from white blood cells, but also from many other types of cells. He discovered that nuclein was slightly different from the organic molecules that scientists had found so far. Up until this moment, organic molecules were known to contain the elements carbon, hydrogen, oxygen, and nitrogen. But nuclein also contained the element phosphorous. Miescher was not exactly sure what role nuclein played in the body, but by the end of his scientific career, he suspected that it had something to do with fertilization.

Miescher's discovery was the first crude extract of the DNA molecule. His extract also contained proteins. Over time, other scientists discovered ways to separate out the proteins and leave behind just the DNA molecule. About 10 years after Miescher's discovery of nuclein, Albrecht Kossel (1853–1927), a German biochemist, discovered that nuclein contained four organic bases—adenine (A), thymine (T), guanine (G), and cytosine (C)—a discovery that earned him the Nobel Prize in Physiology or Medicine in 1910.

A Russian-American chemist named Phoebus Levene (1869–1940) was working with Kossel, and he identified the sugar in nuclein as deoxyribose. Eventually, nuclein was renamed for its structure (a ribose-based, sugar-phosphate backbone) and its properties (its acidic nature). Its new name was deoxyribonucleic acid, or DNA.

Then in 1943, Oswald Avery (1877–1955), an American researcher, discovered that the DNA molecule actually carried genetic information. Before Avery's discovery, scientists thought hereditary information would be carried by a protein, not a nucleic acid. But, by the late 1940s, most scientists were convinced that the DNA molecule did indeed carry genetic information on to the next generation.

Part of the mystery unraveled again in 1950, when Erwin Chargaff (1905–2002) discovered that while the arrangement of the nitrogen bases in DNA (adenine, thymine, guanine, and cytosine) varied, the ratio between certain bases was always 1 to 1. The amount of adenine always equaled the amount of thymine, and the amount of guanine always equaled the amount of cytosine. This led to the idea that adenine always pairs with thymine and guanine always pairs with cytosine in the DNA molecule. This idea later became known as "Chargaff's Rules."

Meanwhile, in the early 1950s, Maurice Wilkins (1916–2004) and Rosalind Franklin (1920–1958) were also studying the DNA molecule. They were trying to figure out the shape of the DNA molecule by taking pictures of it using a technique called X-ray diffraction. This technique shows the structure of a substance when X-rays hit the atoms in the substance and bounce off of them in specific patterns. Franklin thought that her X-ray diffraction patterns showed that the DNA molecule was a helix, but she was not entirely sure. She wanted to do more testing. But in 1953, Wilkins decided (many scientists believe without Franklin's knowledge or consent) to show James Watson (b. 1928), an American geneticist, Franklin's images of the DNA molecule.

That same year, Watson and Francis Crick (1916–2004), a British biophysicist, put all the pieces together and determined that the DNA molecule was indeed a helix. In fact, they proposed that the DNA molecule was actually made up of two helixes—one going up and the other going down. This formed the backbone of a double helix. But the X-ray images of the DNA molecule also showed that the helixes were always at the same distance from one another. So what kept them from collapsing into one another and tangling?

Chromosome Theory of Heredity 45

Figure 4.3 Watson and Crick view their DNA model.

In 1952, Crick had learned of Chargaff's base pair research that showed adenine and thymine paired in a 1 to 1 ratio and so did cytosine and guanine. And Watson, while playing with a molecular model of the nitrogen bases, realized that an adenine-thymine pair and a cytosine-guanine pair would have identical shapes. So in 1953, Watson and Crick proposed that the bases paired up in the middle of the double helix, keeping the chains at a constant distance from each other (Figure 4.3).

Watson and Crick went on to suggest that the way the DNA molecule makes a copy of itself during cell division is to "unzip" the double helix. Another strand of DNA forms that is complementary

48 HEREDITY

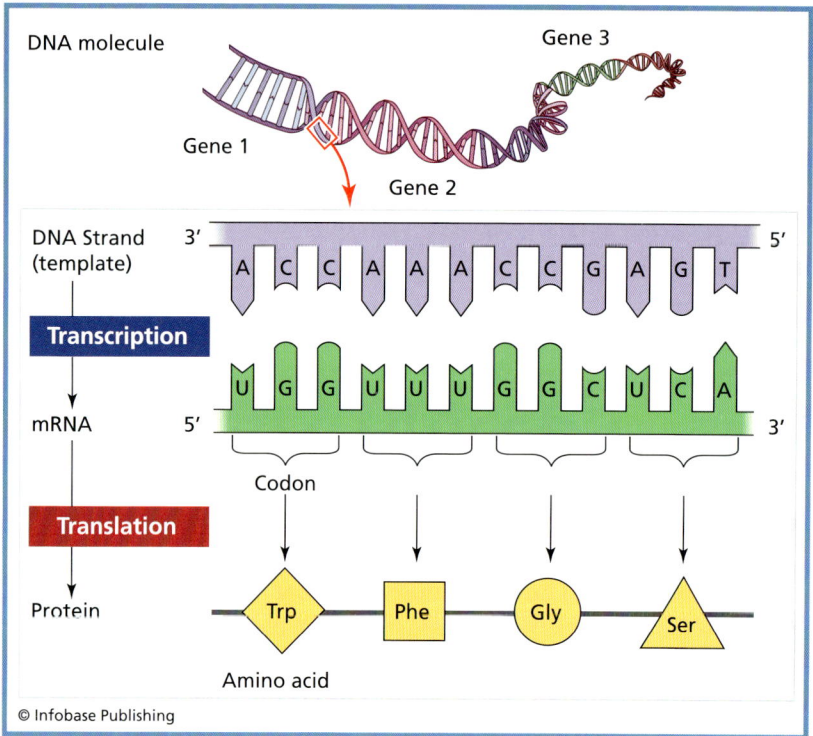

Figure 5.1 Messenger RNA (mRNA) is created through transcription. mRNA acts as a messenger, taking DNA's instructions on making proteins and transferring those instructions from the nucleus of the cell to the structures in the cell's cytoplasm that make protein. In translation, a codon—or a group of three mRNA bases—tells cells which amino acids are needed to make a protein.

The smallest part of the mRNA molecule that means something to a cell is three bases long. A group of three mRNA bases, also called a triplet, makes up a **codon**. In 1966, Marshall Nirenberg (b. 1927), Heinrich Matthaei (b. 1929), and Severo Ochoa (1905–1993) discovered that codons tell a cell which **amino acids** it needs to assemble to make a protein. Amino acids are the building blocks of proteins. This process is called **translation**.

The mRNA codon AUG (adenine-uracil-guanine), for example, is called a start codon. The start codon tells the cell when to start translation. It also codes for the amino acid methionine. The codon CUA codes for the amino acid leucine. And the codons UGU and GUG code for the amino acids cysteine and valine, respectively. So, if a short string of mRNA existed in a cell that read AUGCUAUGUGUG, this string would be translated into a chain of amino acids that would read: methionine-leucine-cysteine-valine.

There are 64 codon possibilities, which code for one of 20 amino acids. Because there are only 20 amino acids, and there are 64 codons, there is some overlap. In other words, several codons code for the same amino acid. Of these 64 possibilities, all but three code for a specific amino acid. The three codons UAA, UAG, and UGA signal the cell to stop translation.

For the most part, this code is universal to all types of life. Animals, plants, humans, and other organisms all have the same basic code. There are a few exceptions, but they are mainly limited to assigning one or two codons differently.

Each amino acid in a protein is called a monomer, and proteins are polymers (long strings of monomers). In other words, proteins are made up of many individual units (amino acids) linked together into a larger molecule. Proteins can also be called polypeptides. Most proteins contain 200 to 300 amino acids, but some are smaller. Smaller proteins are often called peptides. Some proteins are very large, however. The largest one found in the human body, so far, is titin, which has over 34,000 amino acids in a single chain, and is found in cardiac and skeletal muscles.

CELL DIVISION

The process of cell division is necessary for life to function. In this process, one cell, the parent cell, divides into two daughter cells. This is called the cell cycle and has four distinct steps: a G1 (or gap-1) phase, an S phase, a G2 (or gap-2) phase, and mitosis. During the G1 phase, a cell grows in size and prepares to replicate (or copy) the chromosomes. The S phase is the synthesizing phase, when the DNA molecule is replicated, doubling it. Once the DNA is doubled, the cell enters the G2 phase, and prepares to divide. Collectively, the G1 phase, S phase, and G2 phase are called interphase. **Mitosis** is the stage in which the cell actually divides into two daughter cells, each with its own copy of the DNA molecule. In a mammalian cell, mitosis lasts only for a short time.

Mitosis

The process of mitosis can also be broken down into steps: prophase, metaphase, anaphase, telophase, and cytokinesis. In preparation for cell division, the DNA molecule is copied during the S phase of the cell cycle. But chromosomes are not visible in the cell at this time. The DNA molecule and all the proteins that are associated with it (the histones) are uncoiled chromatin during this phase.

When prophase begins, this chromatin begins to condense into chromosomes, the DNA coils around the histones. This can be seen under a light microscope. At this point, the chromosomes consist of two sister chromatids that were formed during DNA duplication. The two sister chromatids are joined at a constricted area on the chromosome called the **centromere**. The chromatids contain identical genetic information. The **centrioles**, small organelles that will produce spindle fibers needed to allow the cell to divide, also move to the opposite ends of the cell during this phase.

During metaphase, these spindle fibers apply tension to the chromosomes, causing them to line up in the center of the cell. The spindle fibers begin to shorten, pulling the chromatids apart and toward opposite ends of the cell during anaphase. The chromatids are now two separate daughter chromosomes.

The next step of mitosis is telophase, during which the daughter chromosomes arrive at the opposite ends of the cell and the spindle fibers disappear. A new nuclear membrane also forms around the two sets of daughter chromosomes and the chromosomes unravel, returning to the chromatin state. Chromosomes are no longer visible under a light microscope during telophase.

Then the last phase of mitosis, cytokinesis, begins. During cytokinesis, the cytoplasm of the parent cell is divided into two daughter cells, each of which contains one set of identical chromosomes inside their new nucleus. Following cytokinesis, the two new cells return to interphase to start the cycle over again (Figure 5.2).

Passing Genes to the Next Generation **51**

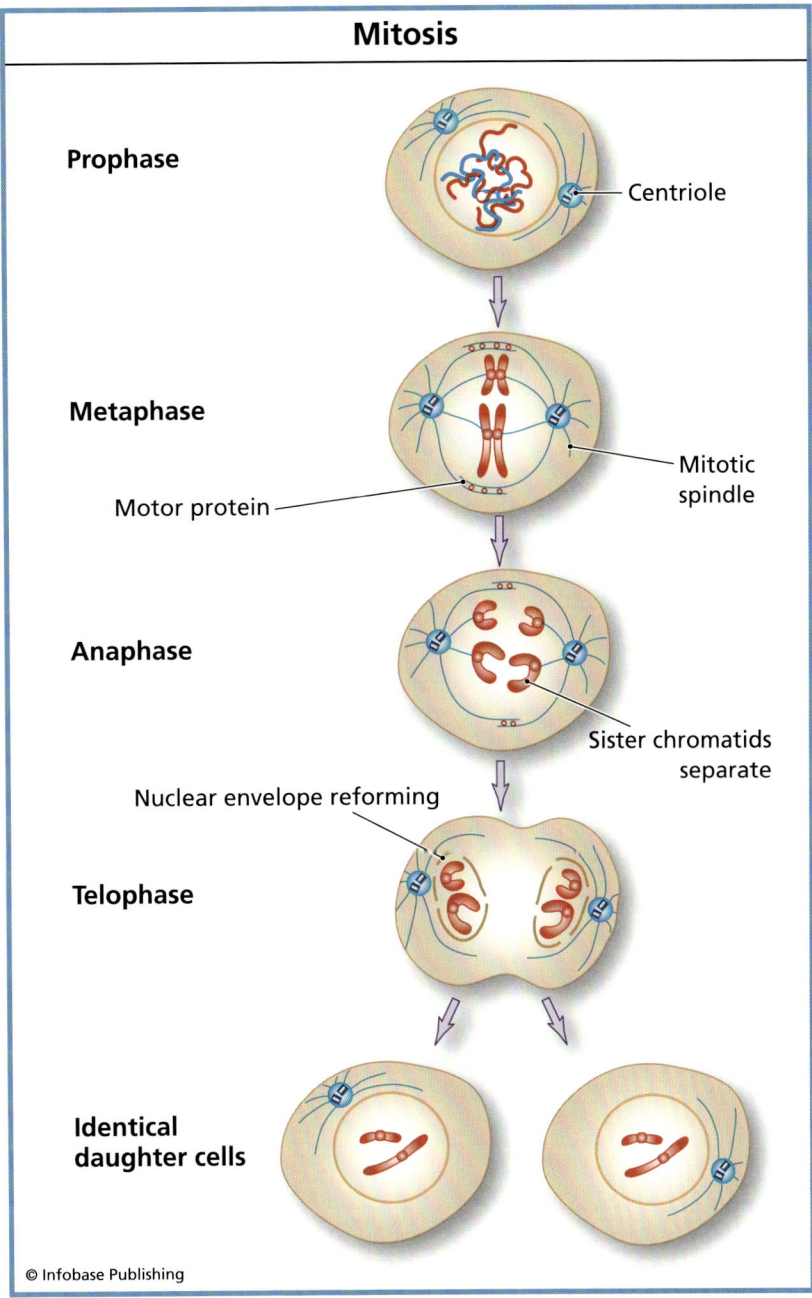

Figure 5.2 Mitosis is when an autosome—all chromosomes except the sex chromosomes—divides into two daughter cells, each of which has a full copy of the DNA molecule.

Meiosis

Mitosis is the process in which autosomes duplicate themselves. However, gametes are produced by a different type of cell division known as meiosis. The process of meiosis actually involves two cell divisions—meiosis I and meiosis II. During interphase, before meiosis I begins, the DNA molecule is replicated just like it is during the interphase state of the cell cycle.

The first division, meiosis I, consists of four main stages: prophase I, metaphase I, anaphase I, and telophase I. During prophase I, chromatin condenses into chromosomes just like it does in mitosis prophase. As with mitosis, at this point each chromosome consists of two chromatids. The centrioles also move to opposite ends of the cell, and the spindle fibers form during prophase I, just as they do during prophase in mitosis. One difference between mitosis and meiosis occurs at the end of this phase, however. Near the end of prophase I during meiosis, sister chromatids undergo a process called crossing-over.

Crossing-over is a process in which two **homologous chromosomes** exchange segments. In other words, two matching chromosomes, one from the mother and the other from the father, exchange genetic material. This process is also called **recombination**. Genetic recombination results in genetic variation between parent and offspring, and is necessary to maintain genetic diversity. A population that has genetic diversity is better equipped to adapt and survive changes in their environment than a group with a more uniform genetic makeup.

After prophase I, metaphase I begins, during which the homologous chromosomes line up in the center of the cell. So, for example, both members of the chromosome 1 pair line up side by side. So do chromosomes 2 through 22 and the two sex chromosomes. During anaphase I, the homologous chromosomes are pulled (by spindle fibers) to the opposite sides of the cells. So each side now has chromosomes 1 through 22 and one sex chromosome. The sister chromatids are not separated at this point; only pairs of homologous chromosomes are separated. Then during telophase I, two daughter cells are formed, each one containing one chromosome from each homologous pair. Each of the chromosomes in the daughter cells has two chromatids.

Passing Genes to the Next Generation 53

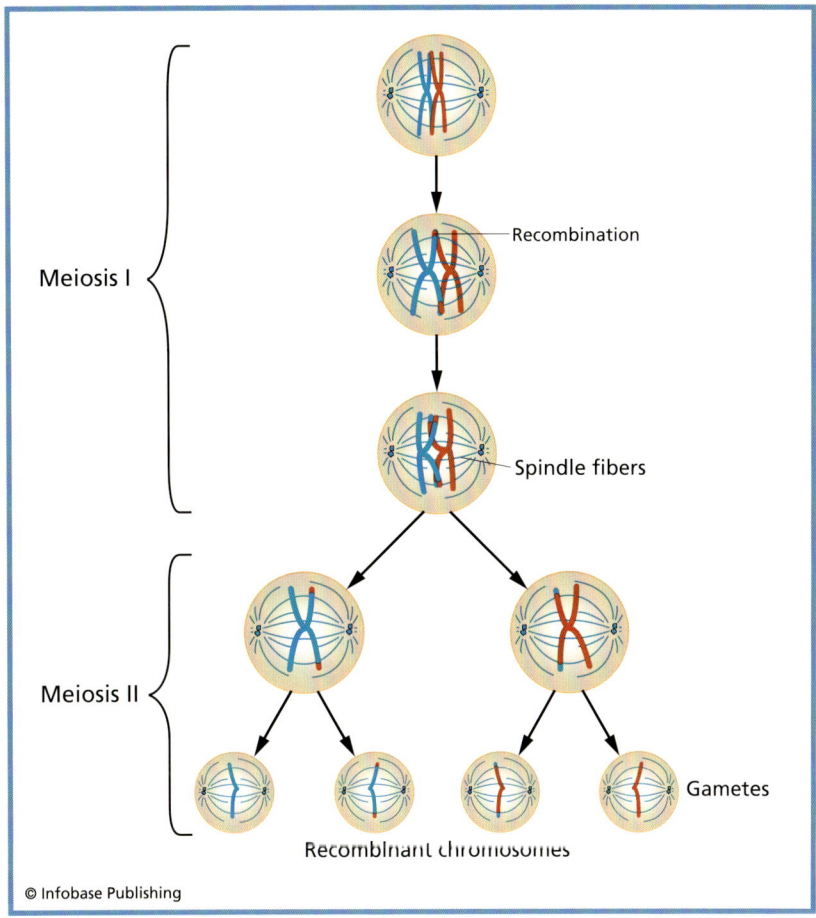

Figure 5.3 Cell division in gametes—or sex cells—happens during the process of meiosis, which occurs in two phases. In meiosis, a parent cell divides twice, creating four daughter cells, each of which receives half the amount of DNA as the parent cell.

Another difference between meiosis and mitosis is that in meiosis, the daughter cells do not return to interphase at this point. Instead, they go through another division—meiosis II. Meiosis II also has four stages: prophase II, metaphase II, anaphase II, and telophase II. Meiosis II is much like mitosis, except there is no DNA replication because each chromosome already consists of two sister chromatids. During prophase II, the centrioles move to opposite sides of the cell and spindle fibers form. During metaphase II, the chromosomes line up at the center of the cell. The sister chromatids are pulled apart and to opposite sides of the cell during anaphase II. And, four daughter cells are formed during telophase II (remember at the beginning of prophase II, there are two daughter cells, so when they divide, four daughter cells are formed; see Figure 5.3).

These four daughter cells now contain only half of the chromosomes of the original, parent cell. A cell that has only half of the chromosomes that an organism contains is called a **haploid** cell. In humans, this means that a haploid cell would contain 23

How Are Twins Formed?

Twins are a special type of sibling. There are two types of twins, and they are formed in two different ways. Dizygous twins, or fraternal twins, come from two separate eggs that are fertilized by two different sperm. Each twin has its own placenta and amniotic sac in which to grow. Because fraternal twins come from two different eggs and sperm, they are no more genetically similar than any other sibling would be. Fraternal twins may be the same sex or they may be one boy and one girl.

Monozygous twins, or identical twins, on the other hand, come from the fertilization of one egg with one sperm, just like in a single birth. Unlike in a single birth, however, shortly after the egg is fertilized, it separates into two distinct bundles of dividing cells. Because the twins come from the same fertilized egg, they are genetically identical. And since they are identical, they are always the same sex. The babies may have their own amniotic sacs or may share one, depending on the timing of the split. If the splitting occurs very late in the mother's pregnancy and is incomplete, conjoined twins, or what used to be called Siamese twins, will result.

Fraternal twins are, by far, much more common than identical twins. In fact, about two-thirds of twins are fraternal.

chromosomes. Eggs and sperm are haploid cells. Haploid cells are also called gametes.

When human cells undergo mitosis, all 46 chromosomes are replicated (copied) and each daughter cell contains 46 chromosomes. A cell that has an entire chromosome complement (for humans, 46 chromosomes) is called a **diploid** cell. Mitosis results in a diploid cell (all body cells except eggs and sperm), while meiosis results in haploid gametes (eggs and sperm). For this reason, meiosis is sometimes called reduction cell division.

SEX DETERMINATION IN HUMANS

In a human diploid cell, which has 46 chromosomes, 44 of them are called autosomes. Autosomes carry the bulk of the genetic material in an organism, but the remaining two chromosomes determine the organism's sex and sex-linked traits.

In humans, there are two different sex chromosomes—an X and a Y. Normal human females have two X chromosomes, and their genotype is 46, XX. Normal human males have one X and one Y chromosome, and their genotype is 46, XY.

Because females have two X chromosomes, all of their gametes (eggs) will have one X chromosome in them. Recall that gametes are made during meiosis. All of the gametes that a female makes will carry an X as the gender or sex chromosome. Males, on the other hand, can make two different kinds of gametes (sperm); some will carry an X chromosome while others will carry a Y. This is because during meiosis, half of the sperm produced will have an X and half will have a Y chromosome.

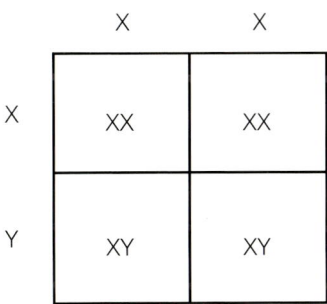

Sex Determination in Other Species

While humans, mammals, fruit flies, and some plants have the XY sex determination system, this is, by no means, the only type of sex determination system in existence. Birds have a similar sex determination system, but their sex chromosomes are called Z and W. The Z and W system is the reverse of the XX/XY sex determination system. In other words, in birds, males have two of the same type of sex chromosomes. Their genotypes are ZZ. Female birds, on the other hand, have two different sex chromosomes, making their genotypes ZW.

Another sex determination system called the XX/XO system is used by grasshoppers and some other insects. In the XX/XO system, females have two X chromosomes just like in the XX/XY system. But males have only one sex chromosome—an X. The O stands for the absence of another chromosome.

Honeybees have an odd gender determination system. Fertilized, or diploid, eggs become females, while unfertilized, or haploid, eggs grow into males. Ants and wasps also seem to use this system.

Some types of fish, alligators, and turtles do not use chromosomes to determine sex at all. Instead, the temperature of the environment determines whether the offspring will be male or female. For alligators, warmer temperatures (between 90°F and 93°F or 32°C to 34°C) result in males. While cooler temperatures (82°F to 86°F, or 28°C to 30°C) result in females. Temperatures in between these extremes result in a mix of males and females. Sea turtles are exactly the opposite—warmer nests produce almost all females, while cooler nests produce almost all males, but again, in-between temperatures result in a mix of males and females.

Since the male is the only one making gametes with the Y chromosome, the sperm determines the sex of the offspring. The Punnett square shows that with each pregnancy, the chance of having a boy is 50%, as is the chance of having a girl.

When Meiosis Goes Wrong

Most of the time, meiosis goes normally. But, occasionally, things do not go quite as they are supposed to. Down syndrome, for example, is a genetic disorder that is caused by an error in meiosis. The error results when a gamete, usually an egg, has two copies of chromosome 21 instead of one copy. When a normal gamete joins with a gamete that contains two of chromosome 21, the resulting fertilized egg contains three of chromosome 21. This is the reason that Down syndrome is also called trisomy 21. At the age of 25, women have about a 1 in 1,300 chance of having a baby with Down syndrome. That risk increases to 1 in 365 by the time the woman turns 35, and then 1 in 30 by age 45 because as she gets older, the chance of meiosis going wrong increases.

NON-DISJUNCTION

Down syndrome is a result of nondisjunction during meiosis. Nondisjunction occurs when one of the chromosome pairs fails to separate correctly during one of the stages of meiosis. The result is one gamete with one too many chromosomes (two copies of the same chromosome instead of just one) and one gamete with one too few chromosomes (this gamete has zero copies of the chromosome in

58 HEREDITY

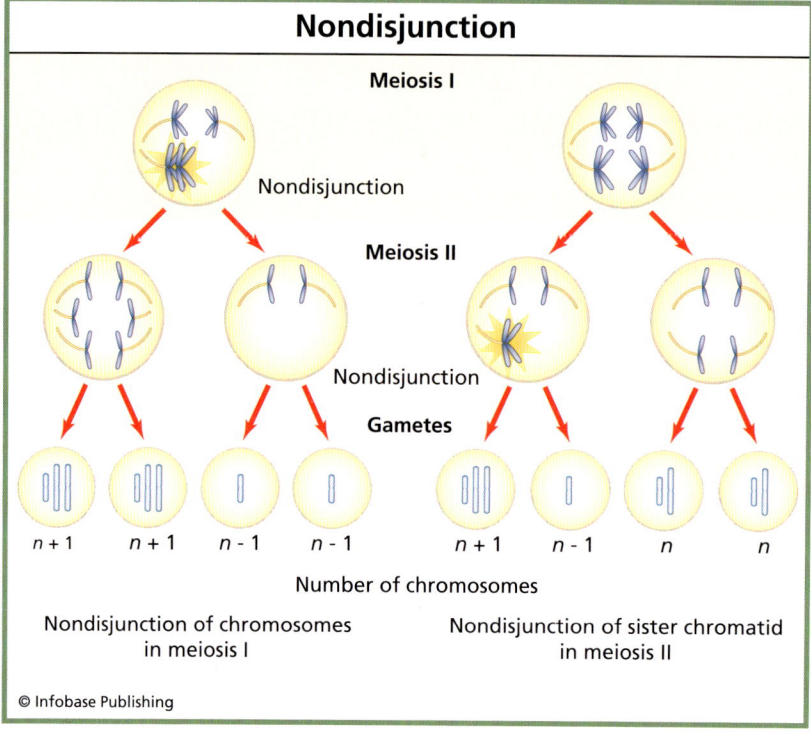

Figure 6.1 When one of the chromosome pairs does not separate correctly during meiosis, the result is nondisjunction. A gamete will have two copies of the same chromosome, or zero copies of the chromosome in question, instead of the usual one copy. This leads to aneuploidy, two common forms of which are trisomy and monosomy.

question). When the number of chromosomes is off by one or two, the condition is called aneuploidy. The two most common forms of aneuploidy are **trisomy** and **monosomy** (Figure 6.1).

Trisomy

Trisomy is a condition in which a person has three copies of a particular chromosome instead of the normal two. Down syndrome is one example of a trisomy condition; it usually involves three copies of the autosome chromosome 21. Down syndrome is one of the more common chromosomal syndromes, occurring in 1 in 733 live births.

The syndrome is named for John Langdon Down (1828–1896), the English physician who first described a group of people who had characteristics of the syndrome in 1866. These physical characteristics include a flattish face, small ears, an upward slant of the eyes, a small mouth that makes the tongue appear to be enlarged, and a single crease across the palm of the hand. The syndrome usually causes some level of physical developmental delay and mental retardation. Therefore, babies with Down syndrome may learn to sit up, crawl, and walk later than children who do not have Down syndrome. The severity of developmental and mental delays varies widely from person to person. Some children with Down syndrome exhibit no other medical conditions, but about half of them also have a congenital (present at the time of birth) heart defect. About half also have trouble with their vision and hearing. Children with Down syndrome have a higher-than-normal risk of developing leukemia, a cancer of the blood.

While Down described the characteristics of Down syndrome, it was not until 1959 that Jérôme Lejeune (1926–1994), a French physician, and Patricia Jacobs (b. 1934), a geneticist, determined that all people with Down syndrome have 47 chromosomes instead of the usual 46.

Two other types of trisomies are Klinefelter syndrome and XYY syndrome. Both trisomies involve the sex chromosomes. The genotype of a male with Klinefelter syndrome is 47, XXY. The Y in the genotype of a person affected by Klinefelter syndrome may alter his or her appearance by making him or her look less masculine. The syndrome is named after Henry Klinefelter who, in 1942, first published a paper describing a group of men who had enlarged breasts, infertility, and sparse facial and body hair. Although all men who have Klinefelter syndrome have a 47, XXY genotype, not every male with Klinefelter syndrome has all of these symptoms. In fact, about 1 in 500 males has an extra X chromosome, but because many do not exhibit symptoms, they may not know that they carry an extra chromosome (Figure 6.2).

XYY males also have an extra copy of a sex chromosome, but in this case, it is a Y. The genotype of an XYY male is 47, XYY. An XYY male results from the nondisjunction of the Y chromosome in a sperm that then fertilizes a normal egg. This genotype causes no significant physical characteristics or medical conditions. XYY males are sometimes taller than their peers, and may have severe acne and an

60 HEREDITY

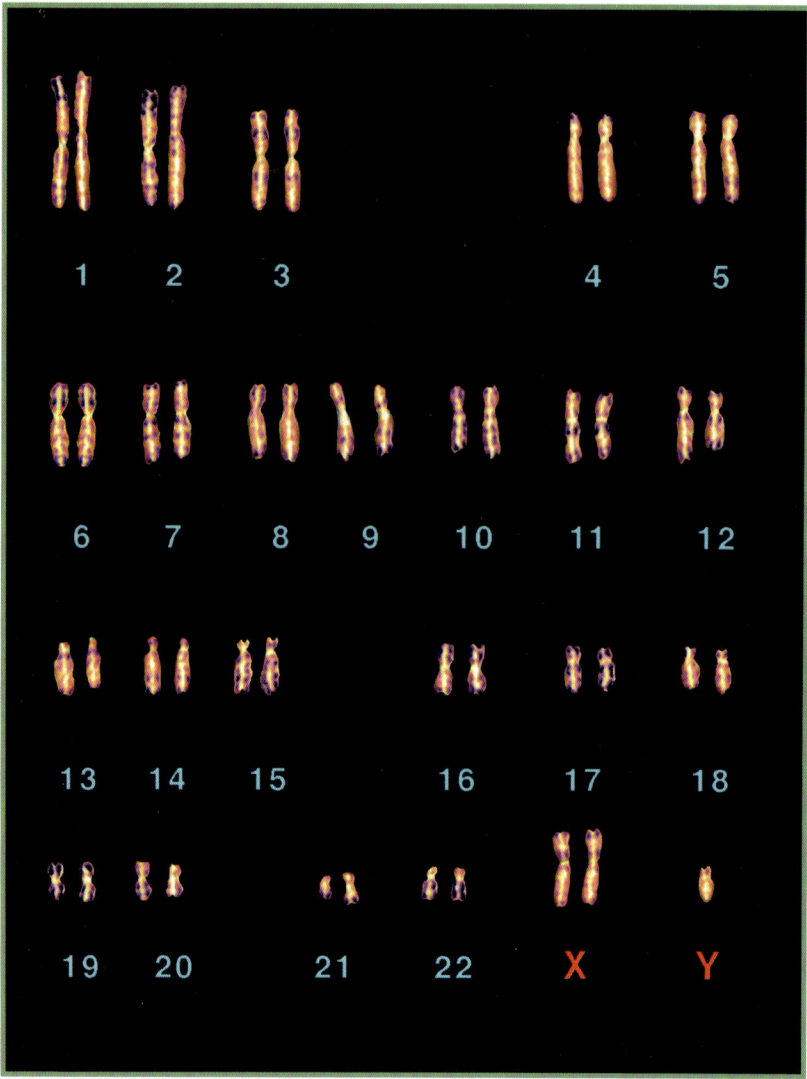

Figure 6.2 A karyotype of a male with Klinefelter syndrome shows an abnormality in the sex chromosomes: Males with Klinefelter syndrome have an extra X chromosome where there should only be one X chromosome and one Y chromosome.

increased risk of learning disabilities. About 1 in 1,000 males is born with XYY syndrome. This means that 5 to 10 boys are born every day in the United States with an extra Y chromosome.

Males are not the only ones that can be born with an unusual number of sex chromosomes. About 1 in 1,000 girls is born with an extra X chromosome, too. These girls have a genotype of 47, XXX. This is called XXX syndrome, triploidy X syndrome, or triple X syndrome. These girls may have an increased risk of developing learning disabilities or speech and language delays. But, like XYY males, many XXX girls have no symptoms and may never know they have an additional X chromosome. Occasionally, girls can be born with four, or even five, X chromosomes. Their genotypes are 48, XXXX and 49, XXXXX, respectively.

Unlike other chromosomes, the extra X chromosomes do not cause much harm, probably due to X-inactivation. Early in the development of a female fetus, one of her X chromosomes is inactivated (turned off). All her cells, thereafter, will have the same X inactivated in every cell. This effectively makes every female have only one copy of the hundreds of genes that lie on the X chromosome, just like males do. Whether the X chromosome that is inherited from the mother or the one inherited from the father is the one that is inactivated is random (except in kangaroos, where it is always the father's X that is inactivated). This inactivation is essential for the female to get the correct number of genes. If inactivation did not occur, females would get a double "dose" of X genes while males would only have a single "dose." The inactivated X is converted into a structure called a Barr body (named after Murray Llewellyn Barr, who discovered them). It seems that when a girl is born with extra X chromosomes, the extras are inactivated, as well.

Monosomy

When one gamete receives both copies of a chromosome during nondisjunction, the other gamete is left with no copies of that chromosome at all. A condition where a person has only one copy of, for example, chromosome 10, is called monosomy 10. However, most monosomies are incompatible with life and the fetus never develops.

The only exception to this rule is in Turner syndrome. Women with Turner syndrome have a genotype of 45, X or 45, XO. The O in a genotype stands for a missing chromosome—in this case, the other X. Worldwide, Turner syndrome affects 1 in 2,500 newborns.

Like other monosomies, Turner syndrome is much more common in pregnancies that do not survive to term (stillbirths and miscarriages). The missing X can cause developmental problems and specific physical characteristics. Women with Turner syndrome tend to be shorter than average, and they are usually infertile because they lack functioning ovaries. Other physical characteristics may include puffiness or swelling of the feet and hands, kidney problems, heart and skeletal abnormalities, and extra skin around the neck. Developmental delays and learning disabilities may also occur, but the severity of these issues varies widely between individuals.

POLYPLOIDY

Polyploidy is a condition in which an organism has more than one complete set of chromosomes. Triploidy, for example, means the organism has three complete sets of chromosomes. So a triploid human would have 69 chromosomes (46 plus one extra set of 23). Triploidy differs from trisomy because an individual with triploidy has three copies of all chromosomes, not just one. One way a triploid fetus can occur is when two sperm fertilize the same egg. Triploid fetuses are very rarely born because they have numerous abnormalities. Most triploid pregnancies end in miscarriage.

Tetraploidy is even more rare of an occurrence than triploidy. But, as the name implies, a tetraploid human fetus would have four complete sets of chromosomes for a chromosome count of 92. Tetraploidy in humans is not compatible with life, but horticulturists purposely breed tetraploidy plants all the time.

Plants with tetraploid genomes seem to have several advantages over normal, diploid plants of the same species. In 1937, two scientists, Albert Blakeslee and Amos Avery, discovered that if plants were exposed to a chemical from the autumn crocus (*Colchicum autumnale*), called colchicine, the plants would consistently develop with more than the normal complement of chromosomes. Daylilies, for example, normally have 22 chromosomes, but, when exposed to colchicines, tetraploid daylilies (with 44 chromosomes) can be bred. Tetraploid daylilies tend to have larger, brighter blooms than normal diploid daylilies.

Triploid daylilies, with 33 chromosomes, are rare, and the ones that do exist are basically infertile. However, research with other

Mutagens

Some chemicals and viruses can cause changes in the DNA molecule. Substances that can cause malformations and birth defects in an embryo if encountered at a specific time during development are called teratogens. Some medicines can be teratogens. Alcohol, cigarette smoke, lead, and organic mercury (which can be ingested when a pregnant woman eats fish contaminated with mercury) are also teratogens. Chickenpox and toxoplasmosis (a parasite that pregnant women can come into contact with if they accidentally touch cat feces) are diseases that are teratogens. Pregnant women should try to avoid as many teratogens as possible, especially during the first three months of pregnancy when the developing fetus is highly vulnerable.

Even as an adult, coming into contact with certain substances can cause DNA damage. **Carcinogens** are substances that scientists either know or suspect cause cancer. Cancer is caused by damage to a cell's DNA that causes the cell to grow out of control. A one-time exposure to a carcinogen may not result in cancer, but long-term exposure to one or many carcinogens probably will. Like teratogens, many known or suspected carcinogens are chemicals or viruses. Radiation is also considered a carcinogen.

Because both teratogens and carcinogens can cause mutations in the DNA, they are both called mutagens. A mutagen is any agent that produces an abnormal amount of mutations in the DNA.

triploid plants has led to the development of seedless fruit, such as watermelon and grapes. Because these plants produce very few seeds, they are virtually infertile. The seedless watermelon, for example, is a cross between a tetraploid watermelon and a normal, diploid watermelon. The seedless variety gets two sets of chromosomes from the tetraploid parent and one from the diploid parent, making the seedless watermelon triploid. So fruit growers make use of the plant's genetic abnormalities and the infertility it causes to produce seedless fruit.

OTHER CHROMOSOMAL ABNORMALITIES

Most of the time, the correct number of chromosomes develops in a fetus. However, just because a fetus has the correct number of chromosomes does not necessarily mean that all of those chromosomes are intact.

Deletions

When a **deletion** occurs, there is a loss of some of the genetic information on a chromosome. This results in what is called a partial monosomy because the genes on the missing part of the chromosome only have one copy instead of two inside the cell. Cri du chat syndrome, for example, is the result of a partial monosomy. Cri du chat is caused by a deletion of a part of chromosome 5. The syndrome is sometimes called 5p- syndrome. The "5p-" describes the part of chromosome 5 that is missing.

The name of the syndrome means "cry of the cat" in French. The name comes from the distinctive high-pitched cries of infants with cri du chat, which sound like that of a cat. This cry is caused by abnormal development of the larynx (the voice box) in the newborn. After a few weeks, the larynx of babies born with cri du chat becomes normal. But children with cri du chat tend to have smaller-than-average heads, low birth weight, developmental delays, and mental retardation.

One in 50,000 babies is born with cri du chat. Most cases of the syndrome are not inherited and there is no family history. Instead, cri du chat syndrome is caused by the random deletion of part of the short arm of chromosome 5 early in embryonic development or during gamete production.

Translocations

In about 10% of the cases of cri du chat, one parent carries a balanced **translocation**. A balanced translocation does not involve any gain or loss of genetic material. The DNA is just shuffled between two different chromosomes. Because there is no gain or loss of genetic material, balanced translocations usually do not cause medical problems (unless the places where the chromosomes break and

When Meiosis Goes Wrong 65

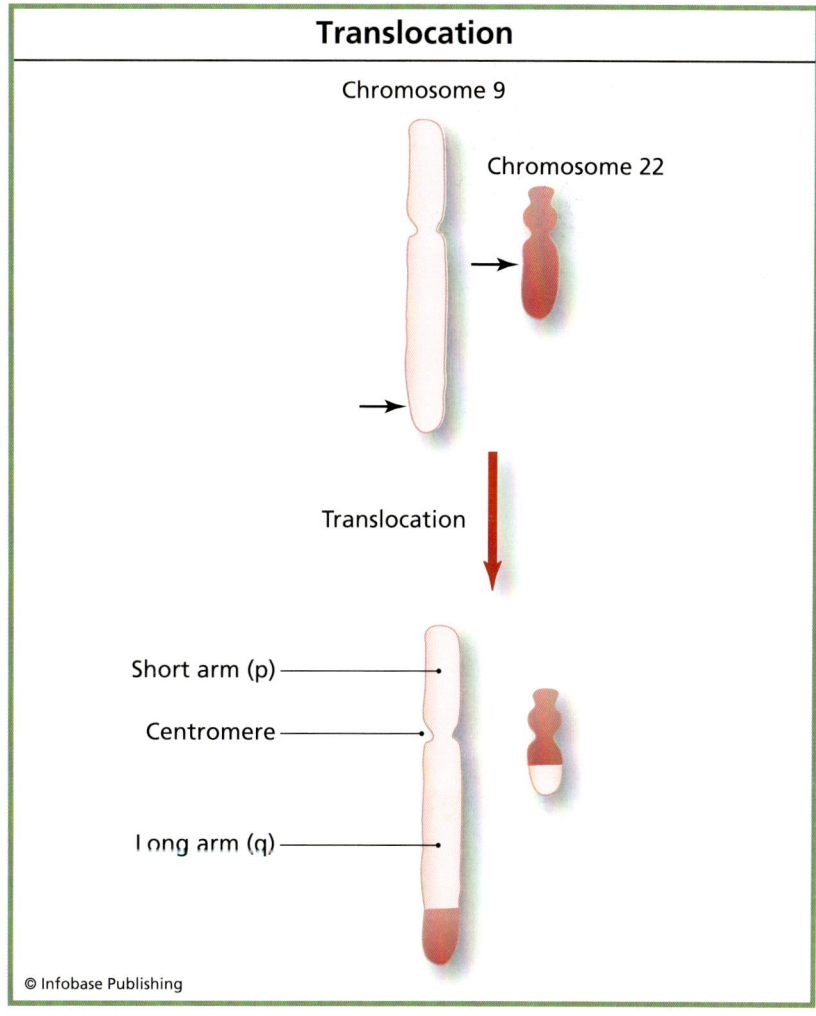

Figure 6.3 In translocation, DNA is rearranged between two chromosomes. Because no genetic material is lost or gained, balanced translocations usually do not result in medical problems.

reattach are in the middle of an important gene) and many people never know they have them. In fact, about 1 in 500 people carries a balanced translocation (Figure 6.3).

However, a balanced translocation can become unbalanced when it is passed on to a child. Recall that chromosomes separate randomly into gametes during meiosis. The child may inherit the chromosome that is missing genetic information (which is the case with cri du chat) or the one that has too much genetic information. Because a parent that carries a balanced translocation is likely to produce gametes with genetic abnormalities, a couple may have difficulties conceiving a child or experience repeated miscarriages. If the couple does conceive a baby and the child is carried to full term, there is a chance that the child will have genetic abnormalities. Not all of the gametes made by a carrier of a balanced translocation will be abnormal, however.

A procedure called an amniocentesis is the best way to determine if a fetus has an unbalanced translocation. During amniocentesis, some of the amniotic fluid the baby is surrounded by in the womb is removed from the mother's body (through a needle in the mother's abdomen). The fluid contains cells shed by the fetus. This amniotic fluid is sent to a laboratory where the baby's chromosomes are analyzed under a light microscope.

Inversions

Like translocations, **inversions** do not involve any loss of genetic material. Unless an important gene is disrupted by the inversion, the person's phenotype will be normal. They may never even know that they have a chromosomal inversion. An inversion is created when a chromosome breaks in two places; the broken part of the chromosome then flips 180 degrees, and is reincorporated into the chromosome. The flipped section is inverted. Inversions can also be thought of as an intrachromosomal (inside a chromosome) translocation. Like other translocations, inversions may produce abnormal gametes that occur due to crossing over during meiosis. If crossing over involves the area of the chromosome that contains the inversion, some gametes may contain only one copy of certain genes, while other gametes may have more than one copy of those genes.

Duplications

Chromosomes can also have **duplications,** which occur when a section of DNA is accidentally copied more than once during DNA replication, resulting in extra genetic material. Pallister Killian syndrome, for example, is caused by duplication of part of chromosome

12. Babies born with Pallister Killian syndrome have four copies of the p arm of chromosome 12 instead of the usual two. Because Pallister Killian syndrome is caused by four copies of the p arm of chromosome 12, it is also called tetrasomy 12p. Mental retardation, streaks of skin that have no color, extra nipples, seizures at birth, joints that do not move, and developmental delays are some of the features of the syndrome. Most people affected with Pallister Killian syndrome do not have the abnormality in every cell; instead, they are *mosaic* for the syndrome.

MOSAICS AND CHIMERAS

A mosaic is an individual who has more than one genotype. The different genotypes are usually the result of an error in DNA replication in one of the cells of a zygote early in the development that creates two different cell lines in the same individual. For example, most people affected with Pallister Killian syndrome have some cells that have tetrasomy 12p in them and another line of cells that are normal. A large majority of women with Turner syndrome are also mosaics with the genotypes 45, X and 46, XX. Whether or not a woman will have symptoms of Turner syndrome depends, to a great degree, on how many 45, X cells she has in relation to normal 46, XX cells. The more normal cells she has, the milder the symptoms tend to be.

Chimeras also have two distinct lines of cells. The difference between a mosaic and a chimera is that a mosaic arises from the same fertilized egg. At some point in the development of the embryo, a cell mutates and becomes abnormal. That abnormality is then carried through all of that cell's daughter cells, resulting in an abnormal cell line and a normal cell line within the same individual. A chimera, however, forms from two separate zygotes that fuse in an early stage of development. This type of chimera is also called a tetragametic chimera because the fetus is formed from four gametes—two eggs and two sperm. If these zygotes did not fuse and had developed normally, fraternal twins would have been the result. If the two zygotes that are fused are of different sexes, a chimera with one 46, XX cell line and one 46, XY cell line is formed. Human chimeras are very rare.

Figure 6.4 This goat-sheep chimera, or "geep," resulted from the fusion of a goat embryo and a sheep embryo.

Scientists have, however, successfully made chimeras in the laboratory. In 1984, the first "geep" was made by fusing a goat embryo with a sheep embryo. Chimeras of two different varieties of mice have been around even longer. Producing chimeras from two differently colored or otherwise genetically distinct mice, for example, helped scientists study how embryos developed. The purpose of the geep was also to study developmental biology.

Chimeras and mosaics are different from hybrids. Hybrids occur when the gametes from two different species combine to make an embryo. A mule, for example, is created from the egg of a horse and the sperm of a donkey. Mules are usually sterile because a horse has 64 chromosomes while a donkey has 62. Mules have 63 chromosomes, an uneven number that does not segregate properly during meiosis, leading to sterility. The offspring of a female donkey and a male horse is called a hinny, but the genetic results are the same.

CANCER—NOT NECESSARILY INHERITED

All cancers are caused by a change in DNA, but most cancers are not hereditary. If genetic mutations occur that damage the way cells regulate their growth and death, cancer can be the result.

Oncogenes are mutated genes that convert normal cells into cancerous cells. Before they are mutated, oncogenes are called proto-oncogenes. Proto-oncogenes are normal genes that carry the information that tells a cell when to divide. When a proto-oncogene mutates into an oncogene, cells can grow out of control.

Other genes in the human genome, called tumor suppressor genes or anti-oncogenes, are responsible for helping prevent cancer. The protein that these genes make inhibits mitosis. When a tumor suppressor gene mutates, it loses its ability to do this. However, a mutated tumor suppressor gene acts as a recessive gene. In other words, both tumor suppressor gene alleles on two homologous chromosomes need to be damaged before the tumor suppressor gene loses its function. Oncogenes, on the other hand, act as dominant genes. If just one proto-oncogene is damaged, cells can grow out of control.

Mutations in proto-oncogenes or tumor suppressor genes can be caused by many things—for example, exposure to a carcinogen such as cigarette smoke or excessive sunlight (radiation). Genetic mistakes that occur in the copying of DNA during cell division can also occur. Most of the time, these mistakes are corrected, but sometimes they are not, and then the mutation is passed down to daughter cells when a cell divides. Over time, as we get older, these mistakes build up, which is the reason why more people get cancer as they age.

Sometimes mutations in tumor suppressor genes can be inherited. But just because someone inherits a mutation does not necessarily mean they will develop cancer. It usually takes several mutations to cause cancer. However, inheriting an existing mutation does raise the risk. This increased risk is called a genetic predisposition to developing cancer. For example, women who inherit the mutated BRCA1 or BRCA2 gene are more likely to get breast cancer than women who inherit normal BRCA1 or BRCA2 genes. However, only 5% of women who develop breast cancer have inherited a damaged BRCA1 or BRCA2 gene. The rest of breast cancer cases are not caused by an inherited risk, but by exposure to carcinogens or just by random chance.

A cancer of the eye called retinoblastoma can form if a fetus inherits a chromosome 13 from a parent who has a deleted RB (retinoblastoma) allele. The RB gene is a tumor suppressor gene, so it inhibits mitosis. In order for the baby to develop retinoblastoma, however, another random mutation must occur in another eye cell that damages the other RB allele. So it is possible to inherit a damaged gene that might predispose someone to developing cancer, but this does not necessarily mean that the person will develop cancer.

Inherited Conditions

A mistake during meiosis affects the way a gamete is formed. If abnormal gametes are a product of nondisjunction, the chance of the same parents having another child with the same disorder is minimal. However, if abnormal gametes are produced due to a balanced translocation, the chance of having another similarly affected child increases. A mistake during meiosis is only one way damaged DNA can be inherited by an offspring. Sometimes parents can carry a damaged gene that has been passed down to them through generations. Many times they are not aware they carry the gene until they have an affected child.

AUTOSOMAL RECESSIVE DISORDERS

Cystic fibrosis, for example, is a disease caused by the deletion of DNA base pairs. Thirty thousand children and adults in the United States have cystic fibrosis, and every year, about 1,000 new cases are diagnosed.

Cystic fibrosis affects the lungs, sweat glands, and digestive system. Because of the gene defect, the bodies of people who are affected with cystic fibrosis produce unusually thick, sticky mucus. Mucus is usually a thin, watery substance that keeps the lining of the lungs, digestive system, reproductive system, and other organ systems moist and protects them from infection. But the thick, sticky mucus of a person affected by cystic fibrosis clogs the lungs, making it difficult to breathe and allowing lung infections to develop. Repeated lung infections can damage the lungs. Mucus also clogs the ducts that allow digestive enzymes to reach the appropriate areas during digestion. This prevents the proper absorption of nutrients and, without medication to replace these digestive enzymes, can affect the patient's growth and weight. The disease also affects the sweat glands, causing them to secrete more salt than they should. This can upset the mineral balance in the body and cause heat-related illnesses.

Cystic fibrosis is one of the most common fatal genetic disorders in the United States. It is more common in Caucasian (white) people than in any other race. One in 3,200 Caucasian babies born in the United States is born with cystic fibrosis. It is an autosomal recessive disease, so both parents must carry a defective copy of the gene in order to have an affected child. People who carry the cystic fibrosis gene are heterozygous for the disease and show no symptoms. One in 29 Caucasians carry the defective gene. If a carrier marries a non-carrier, none of their children will have cystic fibrosis; however, they have a 50% chance of having a child who is a healthy, heterozygous carrier of the disease.

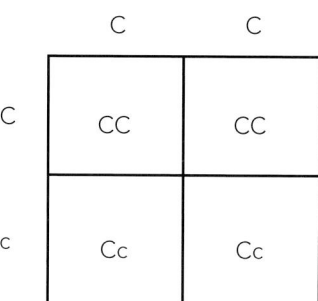

If two carriers marry and have children, there is a 25% chance (1 in 4) that their child will inherit two defective copies of the gene (cc) and be affected with cystic fibrosis. There is also a 25% chance that their child will neither have the disease nor carry it (CC). Again, there is a 50% chance that their child will be a carrier of the disease (Cc) and can pass it on to future generations.

Inherited Conditions 73

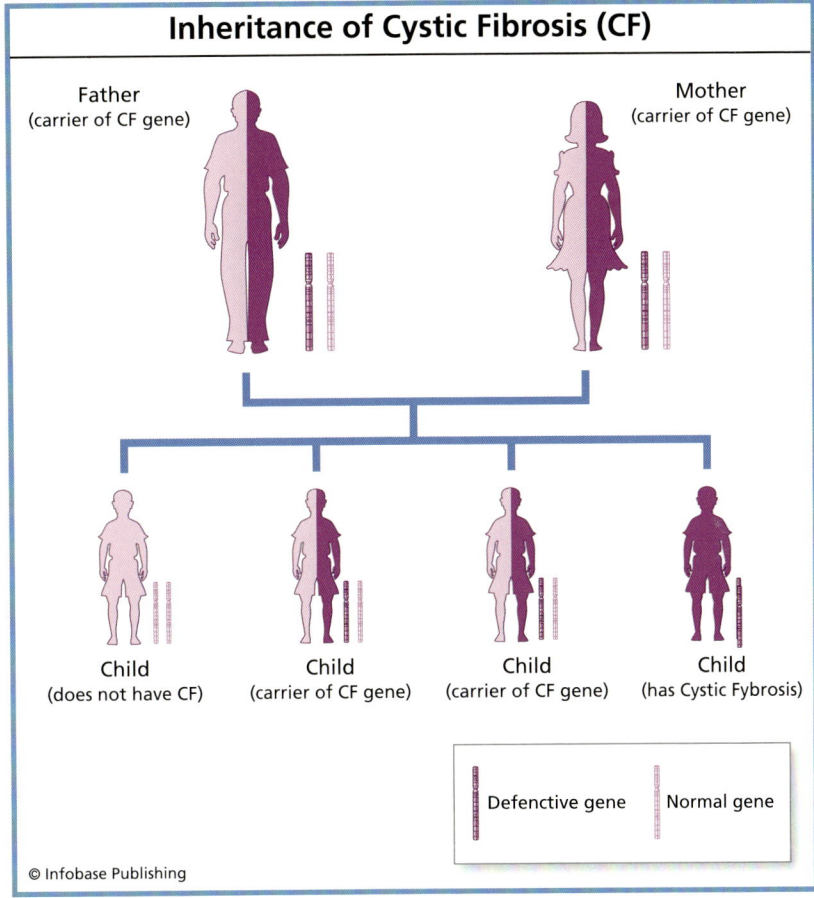

Figure 7.1 A mother and father who carry the gene for cystic fibrosis have a one in four chance of having a child with the disease. There is a 50% chance the child will be a carrier, and one in four chances that the child will not carry the gene at all.

Not only will every child of this couple have an equal chance of being a carrier or noncarrier, he or she also will have an equal chance of being affected by the disease (Figure 7.1).

The gene that causes cystic fibrosis, called CFTR, was identified in 1989. It is found on chromosome 7 and controls the flow of chlorine in and out of certain cells. The normal CFTR gene is about 250,000 base pairs long. In 70% of cystic fibrosis cases, three base pairs are deleted within the CFTR gene. This deletion causes the 508th amino acid (phenylalanine) in the protein that this gene codes for to be omitted during protein synthesis.

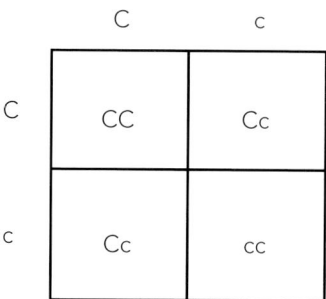

Much research has been done on cystic fibrosis. As a result, people born with cystic fibrosis now live longer and with fewer medical problems than they have in the past—on average, into their mid-to-late thirties. Research continues today to find better treatments and, ultimately, a cure for the disease.

Tay-Sachs disease is another recessive autosomal inherited disorder. Tay-Sachs disease causes the progressive loss of nerve cells in the brain and spinal cord. Infants born with Tay-Sachs may appear normal for the first three to six months of life, but then they begin to lose some of their motor skills, such as rolling over, sitting up, or crawling. Seizures, vision and hearing loss, paralysis, and developmental delays result as the disease progresses. Tay-Sachs disease is most common in people of Ashkenazi (Eastern and Central European) Jewish descent. It also has a higher prevalence in some French-Canadian communities of Québec, the Old Order Amish community in Pennsylvania, and the Cajun population of Louisiana than it does in the general population. Most children with Tay-Sachs disease do not live past the age of four or five.

Sickle cell disease is also an autosomal recessive inherited disease. It is caused by a mutation on chromosome 11 that deforms the red blood cells into a crescent, or sickle, shape. These sickle-shaped red blood cells die faster than normal red blood cells and can cause a shortage of red blood cells (anemia). Also, because of their sickle shape, these abnormal red blood cells can get stuck and clump up in small blood vessels, causing pain and organ damage (Figure 7.2).

Sickle cell disease is most common in people of African, Mediterranean, Indian, and South and Central American descent. In

Inherited Conditions

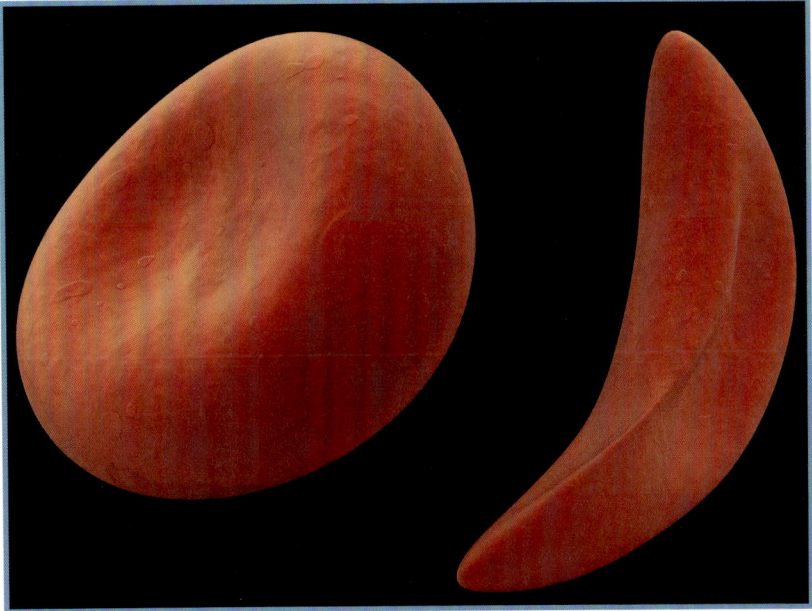

Figure 7.2 This photo shows a regular cell next to a sickled cell (*right*), which has an elongated shape. The sickle shape of this kind of blood cell impairs the cell's ability to transport oxygen.

the United States, sickle cell disease is the most common inherited blood disorder. Like cystic fibrosis and Tay-Sachs disease, a child must inherit two copies of a mutated gene in order to show symptoms of the disease. About 1 in 12 African Americans carry the sickle cell trait.

AUTOSOMAL DOMINANT DISORDERS

Not all autosomal genetic disorders are recessive. In an autosomal dominant disorder, a child only needs to inherit one copy of a mutated gene to show symptoms of the disorder.

Achondroplasia, the most common form of short-limbed dwarfism, for example, is an autosomal dominant inherited disorder. Achondroplasia is characterized by an average-sized trunk but short arms and legs, and occurs in 1 in 15,000 to 40,000 births. It is caused by a mutation in a gene found on chromosome 4. The gene codes for a protein that limits the way cartilage is turned into bone through a process called ossification, especially in the long bones of the arms and legs. Almost all of the cases of achondroplasia are caused by one of two mutations in the FGFR3 gene. These mutations cause the protein to be overactive and disrupt the normal development of bone tissue.

Huntington's disease (or Huntington's chorea) is also an autosomal dominant disease. People who inherit it usually do not show any symptoms of the disease until they are in their thirties or forties. Huntington's disease is a progressive brain disorder that causes symptoms that include uncontrolled movements and loss of thinking ability (cognition). Many people who suffer from it also undergo personality changes. Once symptoms begin,

Mutations and Adaptation

According to Charles Darwin's theory of natural selection, it would seem that genetic diseases such as cystic fibrosis, Tay-Sachs, and sickle cell disease would be selected against and eventually disappear from the general population. So why are they still present, and even prevalent, in some ethnic groups?

In the case of sickle cell disease, scientists have found that children who carry the sickle cell trait (meaning that they are heterozygous for the allele that causes sickle cell anemia) are more likely to survive an infection of malaria than children who are not carriers. Since these children have a higher rate of survival than children who do not carry the trait, the trait is passed on to the next generation. Because they are heterozygous for the sickle cell trait, they do not suffer from illness and death caused by sickle cell disease. However, scientists are not exactly sure how being heterozygous for the sickle cell trait protects these children from malaria.

So what about cystic fibrosis and Tay-Sachs disease? The links between these two disorders and adaptation are

Inherited Conditions   77

Huntington's disease suffers usually survive only 15 to 25 years longer.

Huntington's disease is caused by a mutation of the HD (Huntington) gene found on chromosome 4. Usually a child inherits a mutation of the HD gene from an affected parent, but in rare cases the disease can be the result of a random mutation. Scientists are not exactly sure how the HD gene's protein product functions, but they believe it has something to do with the development of nerve cells. Mutation of the HD gene is found in 3 to 7 out of 100,000 people of European descent. It is rarer in people whose ancestors are from Japan, China, or Africa.

The type of mutation that causes Huntington's disease is a duplication. A mutated HD gene has duplications of a sequence of DNA

> not as clear as the one between malaria and sickle cell trait, but some scientists believe that people heterozygous for cystic fibrosis may have an advantage in surviving a case of cholera. Cholera is a bacterial infection of the intestines that causes persistent diarrhea, and many cholera victims die of dehydration. So how does having the cystic fibrosis trait protect someone from cholera? The bacteria that causes cholera secretes a toxin that binds to the CFTR channels in cells. In a person who is heterozygous for the cystic fibrosis trait, some of these CFTR channels are not formed correctly and the toxin cannot bind to the channel. And since they are heterozygous for the trait, the person also does not suffer from cystic fibrosis.
>
> The situation is similar for Tay-Sachs disease. Studies have shown a link between Tay-Sachs carriers and a resistance to tuberculosis (TB), a bacterial infection of the lungs that was widespread in the Jewish settlements of Eastern Europe during World War II. If not treated, TB can be fatal. Like sickle cell disease and cystic fibrosis, only people who are heterozygous for Tay-Sachs disease seem to have benefited from the trait.

at the top of chromosome 4. The nitrogen bases that are duplicated are CAG. They can be duplicated anywhere from 36 to more than 120 times. Scientists have found that even if a patient inherits a mutated HD gene, it does not necessarily mean that they will develop the disease. If the number of CAG repeats is between 27 and 35, for example, the patient will probably not develop Huntington's disease. However, as the mutated HD gene is passed down from generation to generation, repeats are often added. So, people with 27 to 35 CAG repeats may have children who will be affected by the disease. If the number of CAG repeats is between 36 and 40, the patient may or may not develop symptoms of HD. However, if more than 40 repeats are present, the patient will almost certainly develop symptoms during their lifetime.

In an autosomal dominant disorder, only one parent needs to carry a mutated allele in order to have an affected child. As the following Punnett square shows, if one parent is heterozygous for Huntington's disease (Hh), there is a 50% probability of having a child with the disease.

	H	h
h	Hh	hh
h	Hh	hh

Because the symptoms for Huntington's disease do not show up until the thirties and forties, past the usual time frame of reproduction, many people who are affected by Huntington's disease are not aware that they carry a gene that they may pass on to their children.

X-LINKED DISORDERS

Not all hereditary diseases are linked to one of the 22 autosomes. Some are the result of a mutated sex chromosome—almost always the X chromosome. **X-linked diseases** are usually passed down from

Inherited Conditions **79**

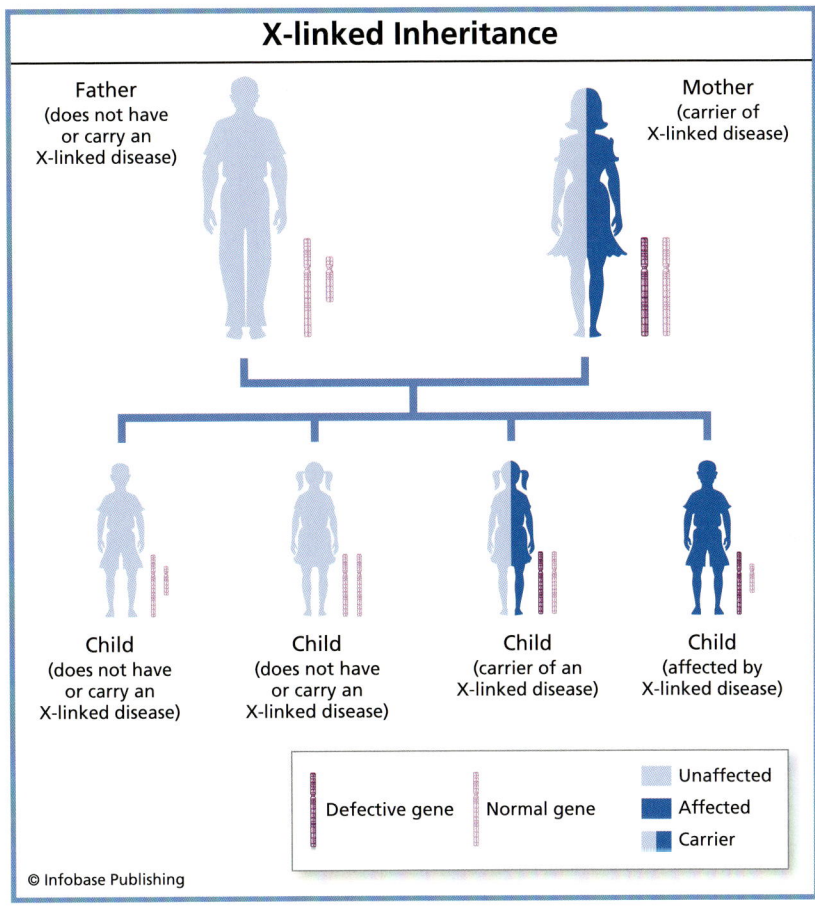

Figure 7.3 X-linked diseases, such as hemophilia, are usually passed from mother to son. If the mother is a carrier, her sons have a 50/50 chance of being affected with the disease. Her daughters will have a 50/50 chance of carrying the trait.

mother to son. The mother's daughters are usually unaffected because they have two copies of the X chromosome. In the first Punnett square on page 80, X^a is a mutated X chromosome. X^A is normal.

Hypothetically, this couple's child would have a 50% chance of not having, nor carrying, an X-linked genetic disease ($X^A X^A$, normal girl; $X^A Y$, normal boy). If the couple has a daughter, she would have a 50% chance of being a carrier ($X^A X^a$) and 50% chance of being "normal." None of the couple's daughters will have the disease. Their sons would have a 50% chance of being affected by the disease (X^aY).

	X^A	X^a
X^A	X^AX^A	X^AX^a
Y	X^AY	X^aY

If the father of a child is affected with an X-linked genetic disease and his partner carries the trait for the same X-linked genetic disease, the couple has a 50% chance of having a child affected by the disease (X^aX^a or X^aY). The couple also has a 50% chance of having an unaffected child (X^AX^a: carrier girl; X^AY: normal boy).

	X^A	X^a
X^a	X^AX^a	X^aX^a
Y	X^AY	X^aY

Hemophilia is an example of an X-linked genetic disease—it prevents the blood from clotting normally, leading to excessive bleeding. The most common form of hemophilia, hemophilia A, occurs in one of about 4,000 males. The condition is caused by a mutation in a gene on the long (q) arm of the X chromosome.

Duchenne and Becker, two forms of muscular dystrophy, are also caused by a mutation in the X chromosome. But this time, the gene involved, the DMD (Duchenne muscular dystrophy) gene, is on the short (p) arm of the X chromosome. About 400 to 600 boys are born with one of these types of muscular dystrophy every year. Both Duchenne and Becker muscular dystrophy are caused by a mutation in the same gene, and both have similar symptoms, which include muscle weakness and atrophy (wasting away) of the skeletal and heart muscles.

Children affected by Duchenne muscular dystrophy usually show signs of the disease in early childhood and are often wheelchair bound by adolescence. Duchenne muscular dystrophy usually progresses fairly rapidly. People affected with Becker muscular dystrophy, on the other hand, usually do not show signs of the disease until later in childhood and possibly not until they are already in adolescence. The symptoms of Becker muscular dystrophy are generally milder, and the disease progresses slower than Duchenne muscular dystrophy. Females who carry a mutated DMD gene may sometimes experience muscle weakness or develop heart abnormalities, but their symptoms are usually much milder than in males affected by the disease.

PEDIGREES

Although Punnett squares are very useful tools, genetic professionals also study family history using a tool called a pedigree. In a pedigree, symbols of different shapes and colors are used to indicate male, female, parent, child, affected, and unaffected. Mating is indicated by a horizontal line connecting a circle and a square. A vertical line stands for an offspring.

Pedigree symbols:

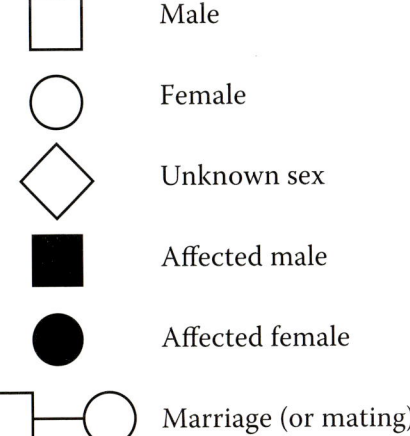

A couple may make an appointment to see a genetic counselor (a professional trained in genetics and counseling who helps families understand and cope with genetic test results) to discuss their family history. In a case like this, the genetic counselor might draw a pedigree, a pictorial representation of the family.

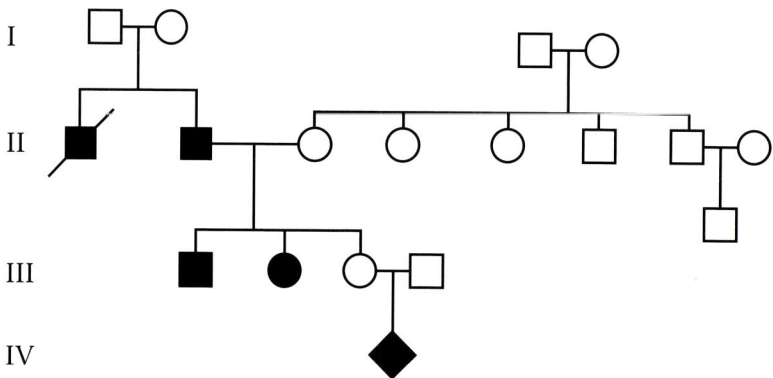

Nature versus Nurture

The nature versus nurture debate is a classic argument in scientific circles. Those who believe that nature determines traits such as behavior and intelligence say that when humans are born, their genetic makeup determines these traits. Those in the nurture camp believe that the environment a child is raised in has more influence on these traits.

The debate seems to have been started by an English scientist named Francis Galton (1822–1911). Galton became interested in the field of heredity after he read the book *Origin of Species* written by his cousin Charles Darwin. Galton was convinced that intelligence and success were due to heredity and that these traits were passed down from generation to generation. He believed this because he observed that intelligent people seemed to come from families of intelligent people. Galton was the first scientist to use twin studies to try to prove that genes determined a person's intelligence.

If, for example, the couple in the third (III) generation consulted a genetic counselor and the counselor drew the pedigree similar to the previous one, the pedigree would show that the female is carrying the couple's child and that child is affected with a genetic disease. It also shows that this child's mother has a brother and a sister, both of whom are affected by the same genetic disease (or, at least, have the same type of symptoms). The mother's father (the filled-in square in the second [II] generation) was also affected. The unborn child's affected grandfather also had an affected brother who died before reproducing (the diagonal line through the other affected male in the second generation shows that he is dead).

> Non-twin siblings share 50% of their genes with their other siblings. Because fraternal (non-identical) twins are the result of two different eggs being fertilized with two different sperm, they also share 50% of their genes like all other siblings in the same family. But monozygous (identical) twins come from one egg. So identical twins share 100% of their genes. By studying hundreds of families with twins, researchers can separate, to some extent, which traits are influenced by heredity and which are influenced more by the environment. For example, if identical twins are separated at birth and adopted by different families, traits they exhibit that are the same (or nearly the same) can be attributed to the fact that they share the same genes. Traits where they differ dramatically, however, are more likely to be influenced by the environments in which they were raised.
>
> For the most part, scientists now believe that a complex combination of nature and nurture are responsible for traits such as intelligence, academic achievement, and behavior.

84 HEREDITY

CODOMINANCE

Not all genetic traits are inherited by the simple rules Gregor Mendel discovered in pea plants, however. In fact, most traits are a result of complicated genetic relationships between multiple (more than two) alleles. Human blood types, for example, are determined by a gene that can have one of three different alleles: A, B, or O. The O allele is recessive. But the A and B alleles are codominant to each other, which means that they are both expressed at the same time. Therefore, humans can have one of four blood types: A, B, AB, or O. A person with A type blood can have a genotype of either AA or AO, but a person with O type blood must carry two O alleles.

If a person with an AO blood type mates with a person with a BO blood type, their child would have a 25% chance of having type AB, a 25% chance of having type B (genotype: BO), a 25% chance of having type A (genotype: AO), and a 25% chance of having type O (genotype: OO) blood.

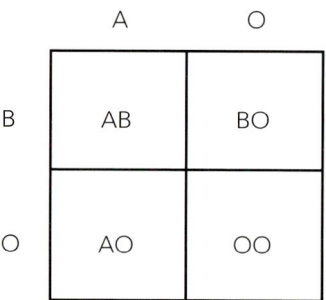

If someone has a phenotype that shows type A blood, they can be heterozygous for A (AO) or homozygous for A (AA). If the family history is known, it is possible to determine their genotype.

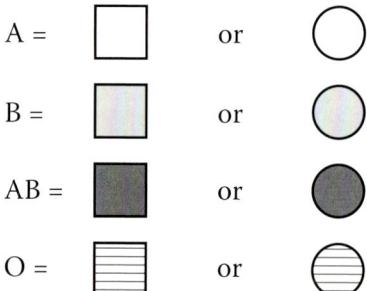

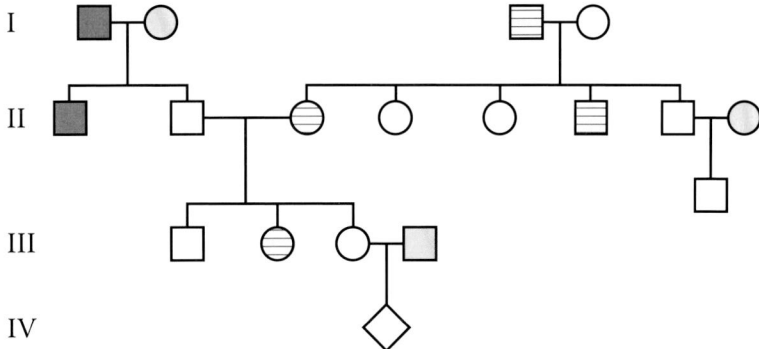

For example, in this pedigree, the woman in the third generation (III) who is pregnant (signified by the unknown sex diamond), has blood type A. By studying her family history, a geneticist could determine if her genotype is AA or AO. Because her mother (in the second generation) has a blood type of O and, therefore, a genotype of OO, and her father's blood type is A (his genotype could be AA or AO), the geneticist sets up the following Punnett squares to show the possible genotypes of the children of this match.

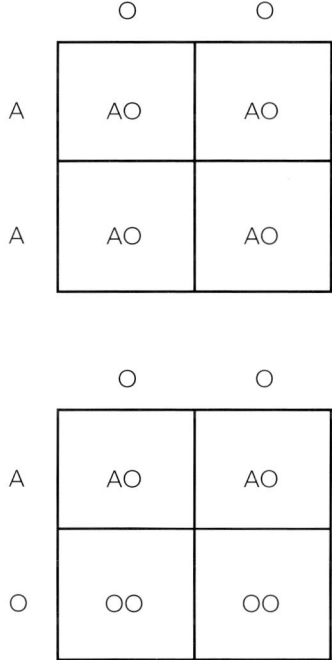

Looking at these two possibilities and the family's pedigree, it can be determined that the woman's father must have a genotype of AO. If he had a genotype of AA, all of his children would have A blood types. But there is one female in the third generation that has blood type O, so the father's genotype must contain the O allele. This means that the pregnant woman must also have a genotype of AO.

Other traits such as skin color, height, intelligence, and behavior cannot be explained by any of the means of inheritance discussed in this chapter. These traits are assumed to be controlled by many different genes, often on different chromosomes, and have much more complicated inheritance patterns.

8

Genetic Medicine

Geneticists have not only identified genes that cause genetic disease, but they have also developed genetic tests to detect these diseases as well as researched possible cures for them.

GENETIC TESTING

Some people who have a family history of a genetic disease such as Tay-Sachs or cystic fibrosis may get a genetic test to see if they carry the mutated gene that causes the disease. For cystic fibrosis, Tay-Sachs, sickle cell, and many of the other genetic diseases discussed in this book, a simple blood test is all that is needed to detect the mutated gene. This is called preconception genetic testing and counseling. If both partners carry the recessive trait, this may influence the couple's decision about whether to have a biological child together. Blood tests and cytogenetic analysis can also detect chromosomal abnormalities, such as translocations, that the parents may carry.

Once a woman is pregnant, there are also genetic tests that can be performed on the unborn baby. This is called prenatal (before birth) testing. Amniocentesis is one of the tests that can be performed. During an amniocentesis, a needle is stuck into the mother's abdomen and into the amniotic sac. Some of the amniotic fluid that surrounds the baby is drawn out through the needle. To make sure there is enough amniotic fluid to take out a sample and still leave enough behind for the baby, amniocentesis is not done until a woman is 16 to 18 weeks pregnant. The test is only done if there is some reason to believe that the baby is at a higher risk for developing a genetic disease because the test itself carries a small risk of miscarriage.

The amniotic fluid can be tested for diseases such as cystic fibrosis, Tay-Sachs disease, and sickle cell disease, as well as for chromosomal abnormalities such as Down syndrome, translocations, and deletions. Scientists in a laboratory look at the baby's chromosomes and prepare a picture of them called a karyotype. They can rule out Down syndrome by counting the number of chromosomes and mak-

Who Should Know?

Who should have access to genetic information? For example, if a 20-year-old woman's father is diagnosed and dies of Huntington disease and she decides to get tested for the mutated Huntington gene, should her insurance company be told the result of those tests? What if the test is positive? The woman and her insurance company now know that she will most likely get sick in the next 10 to 20 years. It is possible that insurance companies could discriminate against people with positive genetic test results by refusing to cover them. Some states have passed laws forbidding this kind of discrimination, but the laws differ from state to state.

If the person being tested is under 18, should his or her parents know? Parents may be able to help a child cope better with the results of a genetic test. But, on the other hand, this information may lead the parents to treat the child differently.

What about current and future employers? Should they be told the result of a genetic test? It might help if they know what is happening in case the employee gets sick while at work. But this could also prevent them from hiring an employee in the first place. So, who should know?

ing sure there are not three of chromosome 21. They can also detect structural abnormalities in chromosomes, such as translocations (balanced and unbalanced), deletions, duplications, and inversions, by comparing the banding patterns of the chromosomes.

Not all genetic testing is limited to before birth, however. People who, for example, have a family history of Huntington's disease can also be tested. And, even though cancer is not an inherited disease, some of the genes that predispose women to breast cancer can be inherited. There are genetic tests to detect the mutated genes for breast cancer, too.

But not everyone with a family history of an inherited disease is convinced that they would like to know what their genetic future holds. Why not? Keep in mind that there is no cure for Huntington's disease and that sufferers die in their late forties or fifties. Would you want to know that you carry a disease that could affect the rest of your life? What if there was a possible cure? Would that factor into your decision making? What if you were planning to have children? Knowing that Huntington's disease is inherited in an autosomal dominant manner, would you then want to know? Everyone has their own opinions and must make their own decisions about these issues. Some people will want to know and others will not. There is no right or wrong answer to these questions. They are your genes.

GENE THERAPY

About 1 in 10 people is born with a genetic disease. While scientists have developed medications and other medical interventions that may reduce the symptoms of some genetic diseases, the only true way to cure a genetic disease is to replace the mutated gene in every cell of the body.

Successes

On September 14, 1990, a four-year-old girl named Ashanthi DeSilva became the first person to receive gene therapy. Ashanthi suffered from a rare genetic disease called severe combined immunodeficiency, or SCID (pronounced *skid*). Patients who have SCID do not produce an enzyme called adenosine deaminase (ADA), which

90 HEREDITY

is needed for the body to make T and B cells (also know as lymphocytes, which are an important part of a healthy immune system).

Before the development of gene therapy trials, there were only two ways to treat patients with SCID: frequent injections of the ADA enzyme (similar to insulin injections), or a bone marrow transplant from a compatible donor. If neither of these treatments worked, the only way children with SCID could live was in an artificial, completely germ-free environment. In 1971, David Vetter, a boy from

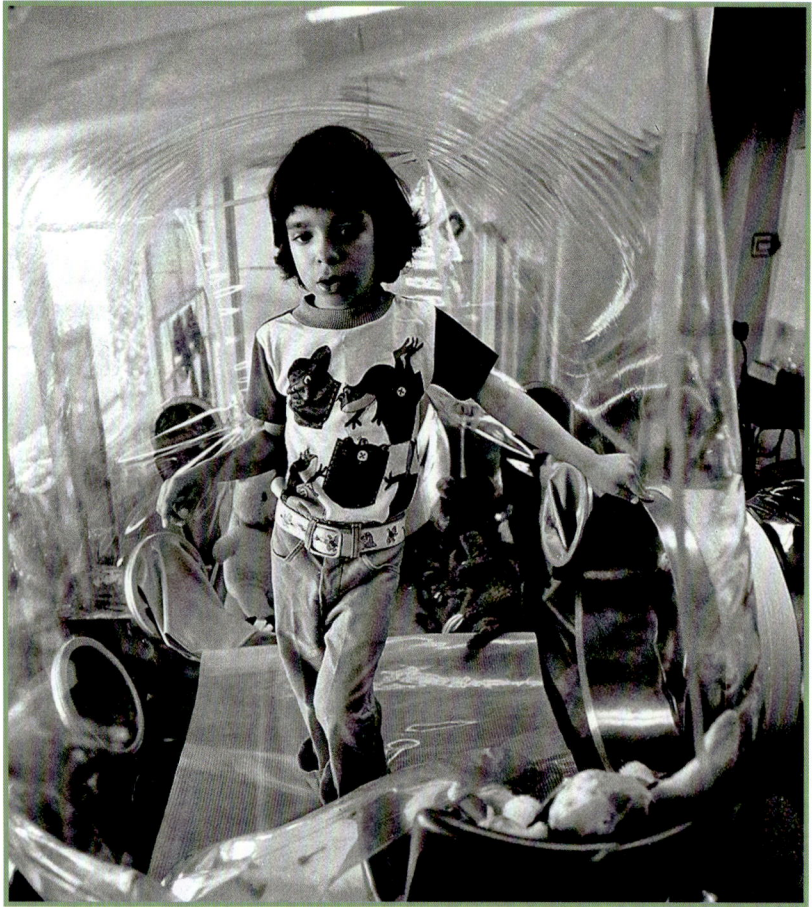

Figure 8.1 Born with severe combined immunodeficiency, which compromised his immune system, David Vetter lived in a sterile, "bubble" environment to protect him from infections.

Texas, was born with an X-linked form of SCID. He lived inside a bubble for 12 years, his entire life, while he waited for a cure for his disease. David became known as the "bubble boy." For this reason, SCID is often called the "bubble boy" disease (Figure 8.1).

When David was born, doctors hoped to be able to cure his disease by doing a bone marrow transplant. In this procedure, the patient's own bone marrow is killed by chemotherapy or radiation and then replaced with the healthy bone marrow of a compatible donor. If the donor does not have a matching tissue type, the patient's body may reject the bone marrow cells. A matching tissue type is often found in one of the patient's siblings. The more siblings a patient has, the greater the possibility of finding a matching tissue type. Even if the donor is compatible, there is still a risk of the patient developing graft-versus-host disease. In graft-versus-host disease, the healthy bone marrow tissue that is transplanted (the graft) into the patient (the host) attacks the patient's body. If this happens, the patient has to take drugs to suppress the new immune system that is now growing inside their body. However, suppressing the immune system leaves the patient open to infection again.

Doctors had been unable to find an exact bone marrow tissue match for David, but something needed to be done. David was very unhappy living in the bubble. So on October 21, 1983, a month after David's 12th birthday, David's doctors and his parents decided to transplant some bone marrow cells from David's older sister into his body. At first, David's bone marrow transplant seemed to be working, but in December of that year he became very sick, and he died in February 1984.

Doctors discovered later that David's sister's bone marrow contained the Epstein-Barr virus (EBV), which is the same virus that causes mononucleosis, or mono. Most people have been exposed to the Epstein-Barr virus at some point during their lifetime. The virus can cause symptoms such as fever, sore throat, and swollen lymph glands. Once a person is infected, the virus stays in the person's body for life and is dormant (inactive). In some very rare cases, an EBV infection can lead to the development of Burkitt's lymphoma, a type of cancer. Unfortunately for David, he had never been exposed to EBV, and when doctors autopsied his body after death, they discovered that he had tumors all over his body. David died from the Burkitt's

92 HEREDITY

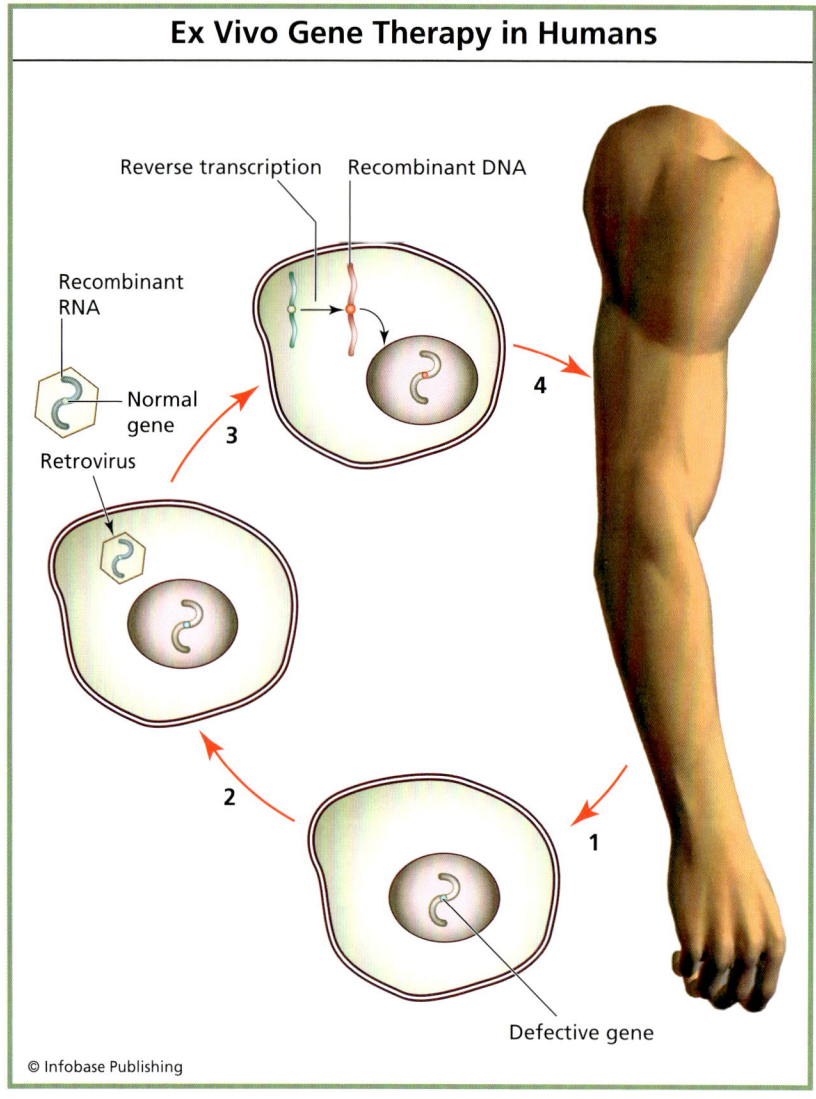

Figure 8.2 In ex vivo gene therapy, doctors take cells from a patient, coax an engineered virus with a healthy copy of the gene to infect those cells, and then return the cells with newly healthy genes to the patient.

lymphoma. His death led scientists to discover that some viruses can cause cancer.

In 1983, gene therapy was not available to David. But SCID was a good test case for gene therapy for several reasons. First of all, only one gene is malfunctioning in the disease and that gene is small. And all of the symptoms of SCID disappear if the gene can be replaced and start functioning on its own. Finally, alternative treatments such as bone marrow transplants and injections are expensive and risky.

To deliver the correct gene into the body's cells, scientists use a vector (carrier). Scientists have tried several different viruses, including retroviruses (HIV, the virus that causes AIDS, is an example of a retrovirus, but it is not used as a vector) and adenoviruses (like the ones that cause the common cold). To make the vector, the parts of the virus that cause people to get sick are disabled. The corrected gene is then added to the virus's genome. Once this virus infects the patient, it delivers the corrected gene into the patient's cells (Figure 8.2).

Seven years after David Vetter died, Ashanthi DeSilva received gene therapy that doctors hoped would cure her SCID. Although she did better than David, she was not completely cured of the disease. As long as she was receiving injections of the correct gene, Ashanthi did well, but as soon as the therapy was discontinued, symptoms of her disease returned and she still had to take medication that delivered ADA to her body. The gene therapy that Ashanthi received targeted her T-cells, which die after a few months.

In 2002, Italian and Israeli doctors figured out that if a SCID patient's own bone marrow stem cells were taken out of their body and the corrected ADA gene was added to those cells, and then the patient's own bone marrow was partially killed (like in a bone marrow transplant), the gene therapy worked better. Unlike T-cells, stem cells live throughout the patient's life instead of dying after a few months. Doctors treated two patients with this method in 2002, and after a year, both patients had fully functioning immune systems. Both patients now live normally. One of the patients was even exposed to chickenpox, a disease that would definitely have killed her before the gene therapy, but she was able to fight it off just fine.

Tragedies

In 1999, 18-year-old Jesse Gelsinger was the first person whose death was attributed to gene therapy. Jesse was being treated at the University of Pennsylvania's Institute of Human Gene Therapy in Philadelphia for a rare metabolic disease when he died. Doctors said

> ## Genetics-based Drugs
>
> Genetics-based medicine is not limited to gene therapy. In 2001, the FDA approved the first genetics-based drug, Gleevec, which is used to treat chronic myeloid leukemia (CML), a type of blood cancer.
>
> CML patients have a translocation between chromosomes 9 and 22. The translocation occurs when a piece of chromosome 22 breaks off and attaches to the bottom of chromosome 9. A tiny piece of chromosome 9 also breaks off and is transferred to the bottom of chromosome 22. The tiny chromosome 22 that results is called the Philadelphia chromosome, named after the city in which researchers first found out that all CML patients carry this translocation.
>
> The breaks in chromosomes 9 and 22 occur within some important genes. When the pieces of chromosomes 9 and 22 fuse back together, they form an oncogene that codes for a protein that causes the bone marrow to make too many white blood cells (which are also abnormal), causing CML. Gleevec blocks this protein, stopping the abnormal growth of white blood cells and keeping the CML under control.

that the treatment triggered a severe reaction, which caused many of Jesse's organs to stop functioning. Scientists stopped gene therapy trials for a time after Jesse's death so they could figure out how to prevent this from happening again.

X-linked SCID patients have been helped by gene therapy, but this has not been without problems. In 2000, 15 French SCID patients were treated with a retrovirus containing the corrected ADA gene. Ten of the 15 have been cured of SCID, but 3 of those 10 boys developed T-cell leukemia, a cancer of the bone marrow that involves the T-cells. Scientists know that retroviruses randomly insert their DNA into the host's DNA. They hypothesized that the retrovirus given the boys with SCID may have integrated its DNA into the middle of a proto-oncogene, causing the boys to develop cancer.

One of the boys died. The other two seem to be cured of SCID, and their cancer is now in remission (not detectable at the moment, but it may come back at some point later). In December 2007, another little boy undergoing the same gene therapy in London was also diagnosed with leukemia.

In light of these tragedies, scientists are being very careful about how they proceed with gene therapy. If they can get the procedure to work, it could mean the difference between an early death (or a severely limited life such as David Vetter's) and the chance to live a normal life for the many people who live with a genetic disorder.

Genetic Technology

While CML is not an inherited disease, scientists hope to one day use the same concept to treat or cure genetic diseases. One step in that process was the Human Genome Project, which could give scientists the tools they need to change the future of genetic research.

THE HUMAN GENOME PROJECT

The Human Genome Project (HGP) was an international effort to map the entire human genome, all 3 billion base pairs of it. When it started in 1990, scientists set a goal of 15 years to complete the project but completed it in 2003, with two years to spare. Many volunteers gave blood to provide DNA for the project. Some of this blood was not used, and the labels on the blood tubes that were used were intentionally removed so no one would know exactly whose DNA was being sequenced. The final sequence, which has been published on the Internet, is a combination of many of the volunteers' DNA.

Because 99.9% of everyone's DNA sequence is exactly the same, having a sequenced human genome has already made the job of finding genes that cause some genetic diseases easier. In the future, scientists hope to find what they suspect is the genetic basis of other diseases such as heart disease, diabetes, and some mental illnesses. Some genes that are involved in cancer had already been identified before the HGP started, but scientists also hope to find even more with help of the sequence. Not only do scientists hope to find the genes that cause disease, but they also hope to develop drugs and other treatments to specifically target these diseases and their faulty genes.

Scientists were surprised at some of the results of the HGP. Before the project began, some scientists estimated that the human genome would contain as many as 100,000 genes. Imagine everyone's surprise when the final estimate was less than half of that—20,000 to 25,000 genes.

CLONING

Except for science fiction writers, no one really gave a thought to the idea of cloning humans until researchers at the Roslin Institute in

Gene Comparison

So how do humans stack up in the number of genes? Well, we have more than a fruit fly. But then again, we have a lot less than corn.

Organism	Number of Genes	Number of Chromosomes
E. coli (bacteria)	3,200	1
Fruit fly	13,600	8
C. elegans (roundworm)	19,500	6
Human	20,000–25,000	46
Mouse	30,000	42
Rice	45,000	24
Maize (corn)	50,000	20

(continues)

(continued)

Scientists have not sequenced the genomes of all organisms, but they do know how many chromosomes others have. Having a large number of chromosomes does not necessarily mean that an organism has a large number of genes, however (compare humans and corn, for example).

Organism	Number of Chromosomes
King Crab	208
Dog, chicken	78
Camel	70
Guinea pig, armadillo, chinchilla	64
Goat	60
Chimpanzee, gorilla, orangutan, potato plant	48
Bat, porpoise	44
Squirrel, soybean plant	40
Cat	38
Porcupine, apple tree	34
Alligator	32
Salamander, tomato plant	24
Shrew	23
Opossum	22
Pea plant	14
House fly	12
Mosquito	6

Scotland produced the first cloned mammal, a sheep named Dolly, in 1997. The type of cloning that produced Dolly is called reproductive cloning. If cloning is mentioned in the media, the reporters are usually talking about reproductive cloning (Figure 9.1).

Genetic Technology 99

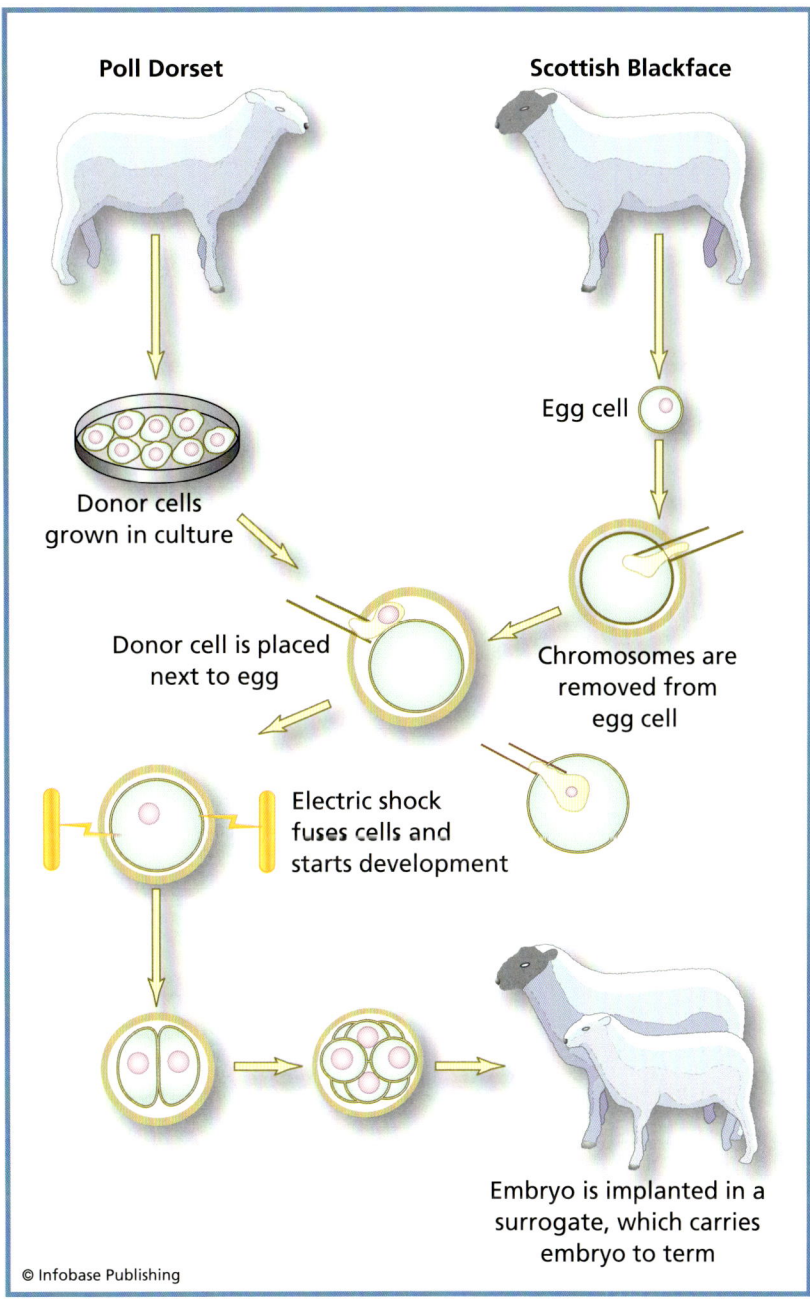

Figure 9.1 The steps of cloning are illustrated here, from implanting a nucleus into a cell whose nucleus has been removed, to electric shock, to implanting the dividing cell into a surrogate mother.

Reproductive cloning is the act of making a genetic twin of a currently living or previously living organism. Dolly was produced by taking the nucleus, including its DNA, from an udder cell of an adult sheep. This nucleus was then implanted into another cell that had its nucleus removed. In order to make this recombined cell start to divide, researchers had to apply chemicals or electric shock to the cell. Once the cell started to divide, the cell was implanted into another sheep that served as a surrogate mother for the developing embryo. This technique is called "somatic cell nuclear transfer," or SCNT.

Dolly's birth surprised some scientists who were convinced that once cells have received instructions to turn into a particular type of cell (called differentiation)—for example, a heart cell, lung cell, or udder cell—there would be no way to reprogram the cells to become something else. It turned out, however, that it was possible to reprogram the cells. But, the news was not all good. Even though the type of sheep Dolly came from usually live to be about 11 or 12 years old, Dolly died at the age of six. When she died, Dolly was suffering from severe arthritis and lung cancer, diseases that usually show up in older animals.

In fact, many of the cloned animals that have been produced to date have suffered much higher rates of death, deformity, mental diseases, and disability than other animals their age that are conceived naturally. Scientists believe this could be a result of incomplete reprogramming of the adult cells used to make the clones. Or it could be due to the fact that nuclear DNA is not the only DNA that exists in the cell. There are also short strands of DNA found in the mitochondria, an organelle that is often called the powerhouse of the cell. When Dolly was created using SCNT, the cell with the nucleus removed still had DNA present in its mitochondria. Because of the presence of mitochondrial DNA, Dolly was not a true identical clone of the animal from which she originated. In fact, none of the clones that have been made so far using the SCNT technique are identical to the animal they came from because of the presence of mitochondrial DNA.

Reproductive cloning is not the only type of cloning, however. DNA cloning, or recombinant DNA technology, is a way to make many copies of the same gene and has been around since the 1970s. Researchers use this method when they need many copies of the

Genetic Technology **101**

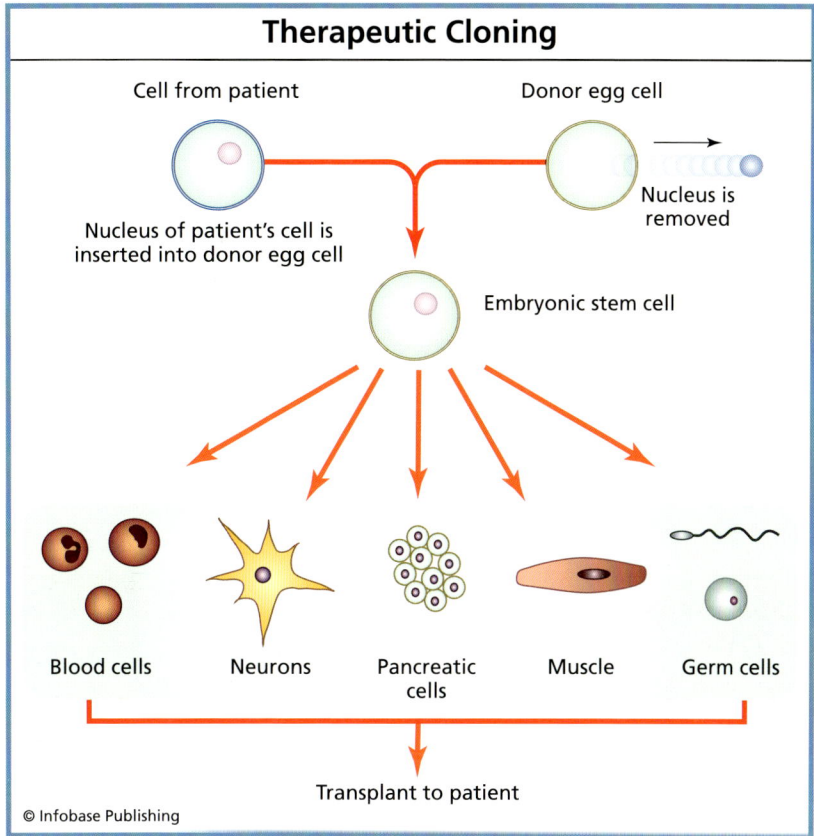

Figure 9.2 The process of therapeutic cloning involves removing the nucleus of a cell and implanting it in another type of cell, where it is then treated with chemicals in order make the egg start dividing. Stem cells can later be removed from the dividing embryo.

same gene so they can study it. The section of DNA under study is usually put into a bacterial cell (although yeast and mammalian cells can also be used). The bacterial cell makes many, many copies of itself and, in the process, many, many copies of the gene in question. Researchers for the Human Genome Project used bacterial host cells to make copies of genes so they could sequence them. DNA cloning is also important in the study and delivery of gene therapy.

Another type of cloning is therapeutic cloning (Figure 9.2). This type of cloning involves creating human stem cells for a particular patient from their own DNA. Stem cells are cells that have not yet differentiated, which means that they can turn into any type of cell in the body, whether it is a heart, brain, or bone cell. In therapeutic cloning, scientists take the nucleus out of a human egg and implant the nucleus of another type of cell (a skin or liver cell, for example). This is the same technique (SCNT) that was used to produce Dolly the sheep. Chemicals are then used to make the egg start to divide. After about five days, stem cells can be harvested from the dividing embryo. Scientists hope that, one day, stem cells may be able to be used as replacement cells to treat diseases such as heart disease, Alzheimer's disease, and cancer. They also hope to be able to grow replacement organs in the laboratory that could one day be used for organ transplants. For example, if scientists were able to take cells from a person who needs an organ transplant and clone those cells, the scientists would be able to harvest stem cells that would be an identical genetic match for that person. Theoretically, this procedure could eliminate the danger of organ rejection.

Even though creating cloned humans is not the goal of therapeutic cloning, harvesting the stem cells does destroy the dividing embryo and this raises ethical questions. Many scientists have expressed a strong belief that trying to clone humans would be highly unethical. First of all, not many of the cloning experiments in animals have been successful thus far. Only one or two cloning experiments out of 100 produce a living clone. And of the living clones born so far, many have had physical problems or deformities, while others have died much younger than their counterparts that were conceived naturally.

GENTICALLY MODIFIED CROPS AND PHARMING

Unlike cloning, genetic manipulation of plants has gone on for centuries. But the process of crossing plants over many generations to produce hybrids that possess desired traits takes time. Scientists can now speed up that process by inserting the genes from one plant into another plant. The goal of making hybrids and genetically manipulating actual genes is the same—to make plants with desired characteristics such as resistance to insects and disease, improved nutrition and taste, and stronger and more plentiful crops.

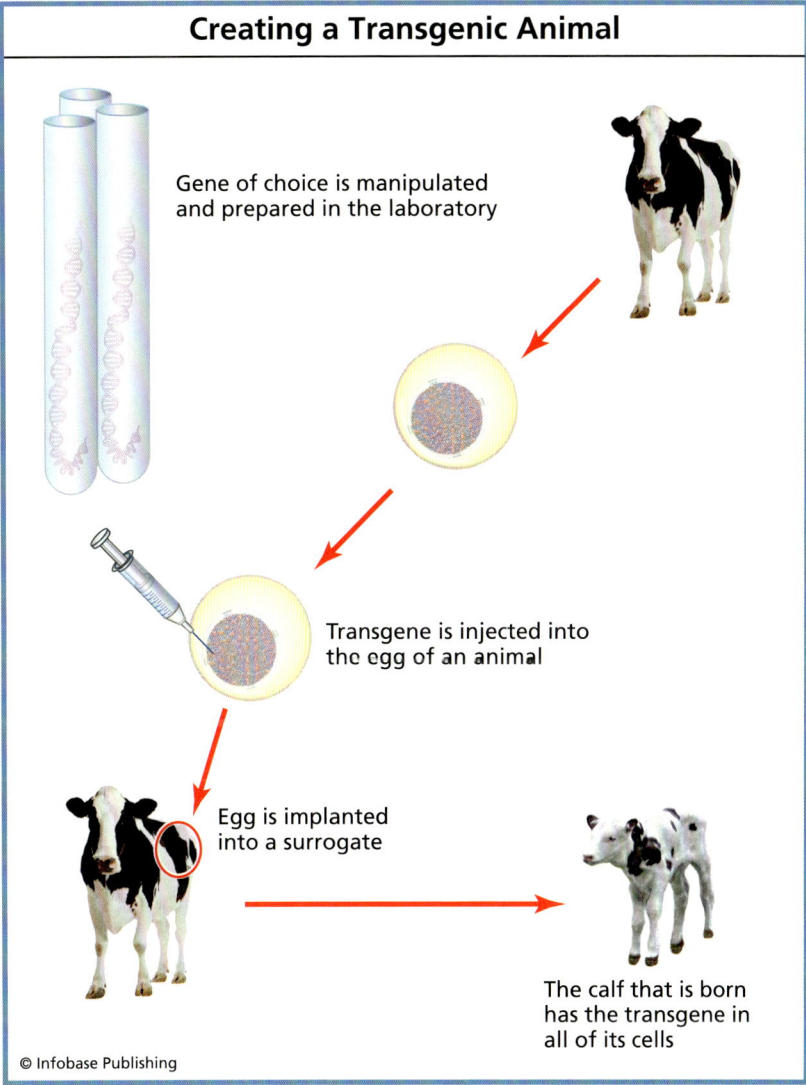

Figure 9.3 Creating a transgenic animal, or an animal that has had genes from another animal spliced into its genome, involves manipulating and preparing a gene in a lab, injecting it into the egg of an animal, and implanting that egg into a surrogate mother.

A type of corn, called Bt corn, for example, contains a gene that allows it to make its own insecticide, a chemical that kills insects that try to eat the corn plant. The inserted gene is called a transgene. Plants that contain transgenes are sometimes called genetically modified (GM) crops. In 2006, more than 10 million farmers in 22 countries planted more than 250 million acres of GM crops. Some of the crops being grown or tested include rice that has had iron and vitamins added to it, sweet potatoes that are resistant to a sweet potato virus, and a variety of plants that are capable of surviving very hot or very cold weather. But scientists are also working on a strain of bananas that can produce human vaccines for infectious diseases such as hepatitis B, cattle that are resistant to mad cow disease, plants that can produce a new type of plastic, and fish, fruit trees, and nut trees that mature more quickly.

Several concerns about GM crops have been raised, however. Some people worry about the unintended, long-term effects of growing and eating GM crops such as spreading or contaminating the transgenes through pollination. There are also concerns about the loss of biodiversity, as well as the long-term effects on people's heath. People may also object to eating animal genes in plants and vice versa.

As they have done with plants, farmers have long bred animals for advantageous traits. As with plants, however, these deliberate crosses to produce cows that provide more milk or chickens that lay more eggs, for example, take time. Scientists are now producing transgenic animals, too. Transgenic animals have had genes from another species spliced into their genome.

Researchers have been doing genetic manipulation for a long time with mice to make animal models of human diseases, but now they are also doing it in order to produce proteins or drugs that can treat human disease. Scientists are using cows, sheep, goats, and chickens for this research because then the drugs can be produced in the animal's milk or, in the case of a chicken, its eggs. Producing drugs for human consumption from animals is called *pharming*. The word comes from the combination of *farming* and *pharmaceuticals* (drug making). Scientists have produced, or are working on producing, human proteins that can help treat cystic fibrosis, hemophilia, osteoporosis, HIV, and malaria. They are also working on animals that can produce certain antibodies that can be used to make vaccines against specific diseases.

Like GM crops, some people have concerns about genetically modified animals. These concerns include effects of pharming on the animal's welfare. Genes are delivered to the animal's genome via retrovirus, so there is the possibility that the delivered gene will be inserted into one of the animal's functioning genes, accidentally turning that gene off. Also, only about 1% of transgenic eggs turn into animals that express the inserted gene in a large enough quantity to be useful. The other eggs either do not form correctly or the animal that is born does not express the transgene. So what happens to these other animals?

THE FUTURE OF GENETIC RESEARCH

Along with advances in GM crops and pharming, scientists also envision a future where each individual has their entire genome mapped. Doctors could then prescribe diet or life-style changes, medications, or checkups designed to keep each individual as healthy as possible based on the information found in their DNA. Scientists also hope to find new medications to treat diseases such as diabetes, heart disease, and mental illnesses, like schizophrenia, as well as other genetic diseases that do not currently have treatments.

DNA MICROCHIPS

Being able to go to your doctor and with a drop of blood be told exactly what is contained within your DNA may sound like science fiction, but it is quickly becoming a possibility with the invention of DNA chips. Smaller than a postage stamp, these chips are made up of a silicone or glass plate that contains single-stranded DNA fragments. The sequences of the DNA fragments on the plate are known. In theory, a scientist or a doctor could put a sample of DNA taken from a patient's pricked finger onto a DNA chip and tell what the patient's DNA sequence is, depending on which single-stranded DNA fragments the patient's DNA sticks to.

Figure 9.4 A DNA microchip, like this one, helped researchers detect two types of leukemia in a 1999 trial test. The microchips, which are generally pieces of etched glass layered with pieces of genes, interact in specific ways with the DNA of whatever material is placed on them.

Who knows where the future of genetic research may lead? It is possible that one day patients may be able to find out during a doctor visit that they are predisposed to developing heart disease, Alzheimer's disease, cancer, or some other common disease that has a genetic component—all before they leave the doctor's office, much less before they start to show symptoms. In the future, doctors may even be able to cure these, or other, genetic diseases. Scientists may figure out how to clone threatened or endangered animals. Almost anything is possible. After all, only 50 years ago, scientists did not even know what DNA looked like—and it is guaranteed that there is still a lot to be learned.

Glossary

Allele One form of a gene found at a particular location on a chromosome.

Amino acids The building blocks of proteins.

Autosome Any chromosome that is not one of the sex chromosomes, X or Y.

Carcinogen A substance that is known or suspected to cause cancer.

Centrioles Small structures that produce spindle fibers needed to allow a cell to divide.

Centromere A constricted part of a chromosome where the spindle fibers attach during cell division.

Chromosome A compact structure made up of the DNA molecule wrapped around proteins making it visible under a light microscope.

Codon Three adjacent DNA or RNA bases that code for an amino acid.

Deletion The loss of some genetic information on a chromosome.

Deoxyribonucleic acid (DNA) The molecule that carries genetic material from generation to generation.

Dihybrid cross A cross in which two different traits are being considered at the same time.

Diploid Having two of each chromosome; in humans, a diploid cell has 46 chromosomes.

Dominant genetic trait A trait that is expressed.

Duplication The repetition of DNA segments within a chromosome.

Gametes Sperm (or pollen) and eggs.

Gene A segment of the DNA molecule that codes for a protein.

Genome The total hereditary material possessed by an organism.

Genotype The genetic makeup of an organism.

Haploid Having one of each chromosome; gametes are haploid cells and, in humans, have 23 chromosomes.

Heredity The transfer of traits and genetic information from one generation to the next.

Heterozygous Possessing two different alleles at the same location on a pair of chromosomes.

Histones Proteins the DNA molecule is wrapped around to form chromosomes.

Homologous chromosomes A matching pair of chromosomes.

Homozygous Possessing the same alleles at the same location on a pair of chromosomes.

Inversion The rearrangement of a section of DNA within a chromosome.

Karyotype A picture of a person's chromosomes.

Meiosis Cell division that produces gametes.

Mitosis Cell division that produces two daughter cells of body cells.

Monosomy A condition in which an individual has only one copy of a particular gene instead of the usual two.

Monohybrid cross A cross in which only one trait is being considered.

Oncogene A mutated gene that allows a normal cell to grow into a cancerous cell.

Phenotype The observable expression of an organism's genes.

Protein Large molecules composed of long chains of amino acids that make up the structural component of cells and control many of the functions of the cell.

Recessive genetic trait A trait that is not expressed in the heterozygous form.

Recombination The exchange of genetic material between two matched homologous chromosomes during meiosis, which results in a new combination of genes in the offspring.

Transcription The process of making RNA (ribonucleic acid) from a template DNA molecule.

Translation The process of turning RNA codons into amino acids that link together to form proteins.

Translocation The rearrangement of sections of DNA between two different chromosomes.

Trisomy A condition in which an individual has three copies of a particular gene instead of the usual two.

Uracil An RNA base that is not found in DNA; it takes the place of thymine and pairs with adenine.

X-linked Found on, or controlled by, genes on the X chromosome.

Bibliography

"A Matter of Sex." College of DuPage. Available online. URL: http://www.cod.edu/people/faculty/fancher/MaterSex.htm.

"Achondroplasia." National Library of Medicine. Available online. URL: http://ghr.nlm.nih.gov/condition=achondroplasia.

Acosta, Teresa. "Hermann Joseph Muller." University of Texas at Austin. Available online. URL: http://www.utexas.edu/faculty/council/2000-2001/memorials/AMR/Muller/muller.html.

"Albrecht Kossel." The Nobel Foundation. Available online. URL: http://nobelprize.org/nobel_prizes/medicine/laureates/1910/kossel-bio.html.

Allen, Garland. "Life Sciences in the Twentieth Century." *History of Science Society Newsletter* 17: 5 (Supplement 1988). Available online. URL: http://depts.washington.edu/hssexec/newsletter/1997/allen.html.

Amato, Ivan. "DNA Chips: A Laboratory in the Palm of Your Hand." National Institutes of Health Office of Science Education. Available online. URL: http://science-education.nih.gov/newsnapshots/TOC_Chips/Chips_RITN/chips_ritn.html.

"Animal Pharming: The Industrialization of Transgenic Animals." USDA Center for Emerging Issues. Available online. URL: http://www.aphis.usda.gov/vs/ceah/cei/bi/emergingmarketcondition_files/animal_pharming.htm.

"Barbara McClintock." National Academy of Sciences. Available online. URL: http://www.nas.edu/history/members/mcclintock.html.

"Boy Living in Bubble Develops Leukemia from Experimental Therapy." FoxNews.Com. Available online. URL: http://www.foxnews.com/story/0,2933,317225,00.html.

Cain, Joe. "The Prince of Peas." *New York Times Book Review*. Available online. URL: http://cogweb.ucla.edu/Abstracts/Cain_on_Henig_00.html.

"CFTR: The Gene Associated with Cystic Fibrosis." The Human Genome Program of the U.S. Department of Energy Office of Science. Available online. URL: http://www.ornl.gov/sci/techresources/Human_Genome/posters/chromosome/cftr.shtml.

"Cloning Fact Sheet." The Human Genome Program of the U.S. Department of Energy Office of Science. Available online. URL: http://www.ornl.gov/sci/techresources/Human_Genome/elsi/cloning.shtml.

"Clue to Why Cystic Fibrosis Has Survived." The New York Times Online. Available online. URL: http://query.nytimes.com/gst/fullpage.html?sec=health&res=9E00EFD6133DF934A35753C1A962958260.

"Converging on DNA." Access Excellence at the National Health Museum. Available online. URL: http://www.accessexcellence.org/RC/AB/BC/1900-1953.html.

"Cri-Du-Chat Syndrome." National Library of Medicine. Available online. URL: http://ghr.nlm.nih.gov/condition=criduchatsyndrome.

"Duchenne and Becker Muscular Dystrophy." National Library of Medicine. Available online. URL: http://ghr.nlm.nih.gov/condition=duchenneandbeckermusculardystrophy.

Eisenhaber, Frank, and Alexander Schleiffer. "Gregor Mendel: The Beginning of Biomathematics." Research Institute of Molecular Pathology Bioinformatics Group. Available online. URL: http://mendel.imp.ac.at/mendeljsp/biography/biography.jsp.

"Expanding the Boundaries of DNA Research." Access Excellence at the National Health Museum. Available online. URL: http://www.accessexcellence.org/RC/AB/BC/1953-1976.html.

"Fruit Flies Illuminate the Chromosome Theory." National Human Genome Research Institute. Available online. URL: http://www.genome.gov/25520245.

"Gene Therapy." PBS Online. Available online. URL: http://www.pbs.org/newshour/bb/health/july-dec99/gene_therapy.htm.

"Gene Therapy – An Overview." Access Excellence at the National Health Museum. Available online. URL: http://www.accessexcellence.org/RC/AB/BA/Gene_Therapy_Overview.html.

"Gene Therapy: Treating the Bubble Babies." Wellcome Trust. Available online. URL: http://genome.wellcome.ac.uk/doc_WTD020936.html.

"Genetic Traits." Stevens Institute of Technology, Center for Innovation in Engineering and Science Education. Available online. URL: http://www.k12science.org/curriculum/genproj/traits.html.

"Genetically Modified Foods and Organisms." The Human Genome Program of the U.S. Department of Energy Office of Science. Available online. URL: http://www.ornl.gov/sci/techresources/Human_Genome/elsi/gmfood.shtml.

"Honeybee Gene Find Ends 150-year Search." *ScienceDaily*. Available online. URL: http://www.sciencedaily.com/releases/2003/08/030822074151.htm.

"Huntington Disease." National Library of Medicine. Available online. URL: http://ghr.nlm.nih.gov/condition=huntingtondisease.

"Imatinib Mesylate (Gleevec)." National Cancer Institute. Available online. URL: http://www.cancer.gov/clinicaltrials/digestpage/gleevec.

Johnston, Ian. "Heredity and Modern Genetics." Malaspina University-College, Nanaimo, British Columbia, Canada. Available online. URL: http://www.mala.bc.ca/~Johnstoi/darwin/sect5.htm.

Kettlewell, Julianna. "'Junk Throws up Precious Secret." BBC News Online. Available online. URL: http://news.bbc.co.uk/2/hi/science/nature/3703935.stm.

Kimball, John. "The Meselson-Stahl Experiment." Available online. URL: http://users.rcn.com/jkimball.ma.ultranet/BiologyPages/M/Meselson_Stahl.html.

"Klinefelter Syndrome." National Institute of Child Health and Human Development. Available online. URL: http://www.nichd.nih.gov/health/topics/klinefelter_syndrome.cfm.

Krock, Lexi. "Understanding Heredity." PBS/NOVA Online. Available online. URL: http://www.pbs.org/wgbh/nova/genome/heredity.html.

Levine, Russell, and Chris Evers. "The Slow Death of Spontaneous Generation." Access Excellence at the National Health Museum. Available online. URL: http://www.accessexcellence.org/RC/AB/BC/Spontaneous_Generation.html.

Lewis, Ricki. "Evolution: Human Genetics: Concepts and Application." PBS Online. Available online. URL: http://www.pbs.org/wgbh/evolution/educators/course/session7/explain_b_pop1.html.

McManus, Rich. "NIDDK's Tjio Ends Distinguished Scientific Career." The NIH Record. Available online. URL: http://www.nih.gov/news/NIH-Record/02_11_97/story01.htm.

McVicker, Steve. "Bursting the Bubble." *Houston Press*. Available online. URL: http://www.houstonpress.com/1997-04-10/news/bursting-the-bubble/1.

"More about Johann Friedrich Miescher." Albert and Mary Lasker Foundation. Available online. URL: http://www.laskerfoundation.org/rprimers/gnn/timeline/1869a.html.

Morreale, S. J., and G.J. Ruiz. "Temperature-dependent Sex Determination: Current Practices Threaten Conservation of Sea Turtles." *Science*. Available online. URL: http://www.sciencemag.org/cgi/content/abstract/216/4551/1245.

Morelle, Rebecca. "Of Mice and Men." BBC News Online. Available online. URL: http://news.bbc.co.uk/1/hi/health/6107796.stm.

"Mosaicism and Chimerism." Colorado State University. Available online. URL: http://www.vivo.colostate.edu/hbooks/genetics/medgen/chromo/mosaics.html.

Newberger, David. "Down Syndrome: Prenatal Risk Assessment and Diagnosis." *American Family Physician*. Available online. URL: http://www.aafp.org/afp/20000815/825.html.

Pajerski, Lauren. "Alligator Mississippiensis." University of Michigan Museum of Zoology. Available online. URL: http://animaldiversity.ummz.umich.edu/site/accounts/information/Alligator_mississippiensis.html.

Phillips, Tony. "The Fruit Fly in You." National Aeronautics and Space Administration. Available online. URL: http://science.nasa.gov/headlines/y2004/03feb_fruitfly.htm.

"Profiles in Science: The Oswald T. Avery Collection." National Library of Medicine. Available online. URL: http://profiles.nlm.nih.gov/CC/.

"Protective Effect of Sickle Cell Trait against Malaria–Associated Mortality and Morbidity." Centers for Disease Control and Prevention. Available online. URL: http://www.cdc.gov/malaria/biology/sicklecell.htm.

"Rediscovery of Mendel's Work." National Human Genome Research Institute. Available online. URL: http://www.genome.gov/25520238.

"Scientists Downsize the Human Genome." MSNBC Online. Available online. URL: http://www.msnbc.msn.com/id/6289901/.

"Seedless Fruits and Vegetables." eNotes.com. URL: http://www.enotes.com/how-products-encyclopedia/seedless-fruits-vegetables.

"Sex Determination and Sex Chromosomes." Andrews University. Available online. URL: http://www.biol.andrews.edu/gen/l7.htm.

"Sickle Cell Anemia." The Human Genome Program of the U.S. Department of Energy Office of Science. Available online. URL: http://www.ornl.gov/sci/techresources/Human_Genome/posters/chromosome/sca.shtml.

Taubes, Gary. "The 'Fly People' Make History." Howard Hughes Medical Institute. Available online. URL: http://www.hhmi.org/genesweshare/b100.html.

"Tay-Sachs Disease." National Library of Medicine. Available online. URL: http://ghr.nlm.nih.gov/condition=taysachsdisease.

"The Human Genome Project Completion: Frequently Asked Questions." National Human Genome Research Institute. Available online. URL: http://www.genome.gov/11006943.

"Thomas H. Morgan." The Nobel Foundation. Available online. URL: http://nobelprize.org/nobel_prizes/medicine/laureates/1933/morgan-bio.html.

"Turner Syndrome." National Library of Medicine. Available online. URL: http://ghr.nlm.nih.gov/condition=turnersyndrome.

"Watson and Crick Describe Structure of DNA." PBS Online. Available online. URL: http://www.pbs.org/wgbh/aso/databank/entries/do53dn.html.

"What is the Difference Between Diploid and Tetraploid Daylilies?" The American Hemerocallis Society. Available online. URL: http://www.daylilies.org/AHSfaq1.html#diff.

Wiegand, Susan. "William Harvey." Access Excellence at the National Health Museum. Available online. URL: http://www.accessexcellence.org/RC/AB/BC/William_Harvey.html.

Further Resources

Claybourne, Anna. *Genetics* (Science in Focus Series). New York: Chelsea House Publishers, 2006.

Fullick, Ann. *Inheritance and Selection*. Chicago, Ill.: Heinemann Library, 2006.

Gay, Kathlyn. *Superfood or Superthreat: The Issue of Genetically Engineered Food*. Berkeley Heights, N.J.: Enslow Publishers, 2007.

Hasan, Heather. *Mendel and the Laws of Genetics*. New York: Rosen Publishing Group, 2005.

Morgan, Sally. *From Mendel's Peas to Genetic Fingerprinting: Discovering Inheritance*. Chicago, Ill.: Heinemann Library, 2007.

Pasachoff, Naomi. *Barbara McClintock: Genius of Genetics*. Berkeley Heights, N.J.: Enslow Publishers, 2006.

Phelan, Glen. *Double Helix: The Quest to Uncover the Structure of DNA*. Washington, D.C.: National Geographic Society, 2006.

Schacter, Bernice. *Genetics in the News*. New York: Chelsea House Publishers, 2007.

Stille, Darlene, and Carol Ryback. *Heredity*. Milwaukee, Wis.: Gareth Stevens Pub., 2007.

Web Sites

Cloning in Focus
http://learn.genetics.utah.edu/units/cloning/.

The Gene School
http://library.thinkquest.org/19037/heredity.html.

Genetics Kid Style
http://library.thinkquest.org/3696/index2.htm.

GlaxoSmithKline's Kids Genetics Page
http://www.genetics.gsk.com/kids/index_kids.htm.

Kids Health for Kids (search for keywords such as *genetics, heredity, cystic fibrosis,* etc.)
http://kidshealth.org/kid/.

Tiki's Guide to Genetic Engineering
http://tiki.oneworld.net/penguin/genetics/home.html.

University of Utah Genetic Science Learning Center
http://learn.genetics.utah.edu/.

Picture Credits

Page

8: © Infobase Publishing
11: © Infobase Publishing
12: © Infobase Publishing
19: © Infobase Publishing
22: © Biophoto Associates/
　　Photo Researchers, Inc.
25: © Infobase Publishing
32: © Infobase Publishing
39: © Dr. Jeremy Burgess/
　　Photo Researchers, Inc.
42: Keith Weller/Agricultural
　　Research Service/US
　　Department of Agriculture
45: © A. Barrington Brown/
　　Photo Researchers, Inc.
48: © Infobase Publishing
51: © Infobase Publishing
53: © Infobase Publishing
58: © Infobase Publishing
60: © ISM / Phototake
65: © Infobase Publishing
68: © Geoff Tompkinson/
　　Photo Researchers, Inc.
73: © Infobase Publishing
75: © Sebastian Kaulitzki/
　　Shutterstock
79: © Infobase Publishing
90: © AP Images
92: © Infobase Publishing
99: © Infobase Publishing
101: © Infobase Publishing
103: © Infobase Publishing
106: © dra_schwartz/
　　iStockphoto

Index

A

achondroplasia, 75–76
adenine, 7, 43, 44, 47
alleles, 10, 34
alligators, sex determination in, 56
amino acids, 48
amniocentesis, 66, 87–88
ancient theories of heredity, 16–23
aneuploidy, 58
animals, genetically modified, 104–105. *See also* cloning
anti-oncogenes, 69
Aristotle, 16–17
autosomal dominant disorders, 75–78
autosomal recessive disorders, 71–75
autosomes, 46, 55
Avery, Amos, 62
Avery, Oswald, 44

B

balanced translocation, 64–66, 71
Barr body, 61
Barr, Murray Llewellyn, 61
Becker muscular dystrophy, 80–81
birds, sex determination in, 56
Blakeslee, Albert, 62
blood types, human, 84–86
bone marrow transplants, 90–91
breast cancer, tumor suppressor genes and, 69
Bt corn, 104
bubble boy, 90–91
Burkitt's lymphoma, 91–92

C

cancer
 mutagens and, 63
 mutations and, 69–70
carcinogens, 63
Caspersson, Torbjörn, 46
cell division, 49–55
 meiosis, 13, 52–54
 mitosis, 50–51
cells, role of DNA in, 7
centrioles, 50
centromere, 50
CFTR gene, 73–74
Chargaff, Erwin, 44, 45
Chargaff's Rules, 44
chimeras, 67–68
cholera, 77
chromosome abnormalities
 in cancer development, 69–70
 chimeras, 67–68
 deletions and, 64
 duplications and, 66–67
 inversions and, 66
 monosomy, 58, 61–62
 mosaics, 67
 mutagens and, 63
non-disjunction and, 57–58, 71
polyploidy, 62–63
translocations and, 64–66, 71
trisomy, 58–61
chromosomes, 10–13, 38, 46
chronic myeloid leukemia (CML), 94
cloning, 97–102
CML (chronic myeloid leukemia), 94
codominance, 83–86
codon, 48
colchicine, 62
conjoined twins, 54
corn (maize), 40–43, 104
Correns, Carl, 36
cri du chat syndrome, 64
Crick, Francis, 44–46
crops, genetically modified, 102–104
cystic fibrosis, 71–74, 76–77
cytogenetics, 46
cytokinesis, 50
cytosine, 7, 43, 44, 47

D

Darwin, Charles, 21–23, 76, 82
daylilies, tetraploid, 62
de Vries, Hugo, 36
deletions, 64
deoxyribonucleic acid. *See* DNA (deoxyribonucleic acid)

DeSilva, Ashanthi, 89, 93
dihybrid cross, 34–37
dimples, 13–14
diploid cells, 54
dizygous twins. *See* fraternal twins
DNA (deoxyribonucleic acid)
   cloning of, 100–101
   discovery of structure of, 43–46
   human, 8–9
   junk or noncoding, 9
   mitochondrial, 100
   role in cell functioning, 7
DNA microchips, 105–106
Dolly, the cloned sheep, 98, 100
dominant disorders, autosomal, 75–78
dominant genetic traits, 13–14
Down, John Langdon, 59
Down syndrome, 46, 57, 58–59, 88–89
Drosophila melanogaster. *See* fruit fly (*Drosophila melanogaster*)
drugs
   genetically modified animals for production of, 104–105
   genetics-based, 94
Duchenne muscular dystrophy, 80–81
duplications, 66–67
dwarfism, 75–76

E

Empedocles, 16
Epstein-Barr virus, 91
ethical issues
   in genetic testing, 88
   in genetically modified crops, 104
   in pharming, 105
   in stem cell use, 102
eye, cancer of, 70

F

F_1 (first filial generation), 26
F_2 (second filial generation), 27
first filial generation (F_1), 26
5p- syndrome, 64
Franklin, Rosalind, 44, 46
fraternal twins, 54, 83
fruit fly (*Drosophila melanogaster*)
   eye color in, 38
   genetic map of, 38
   genetic mutations in, 39–40
   in genetic research, 40–41

G

Galton, Francis, 82
gametes, 30, 52, 55–56
"geep" chimera, 68
Gelsinger, Jesse, 93–94
gemmules, 21–23
gene comparison, 97–98
gene therapy
   failures, 93–95
   successes, 89–93
genes, 10
genetic counseling, 81–83, 87–89
genetic diversity, 23, 52
genetic map, of fruit fly, 38
genetic mutations
   carcinogens and, 69
   X-ray radiation and, 39–40
genetic research
   fruit fly in, 40–41
   future of, 105–106
   Human Genome Project and, 96–97
genetic testing, 87–89
genetically modified (GM) crops, 102–104
genetics-based drugs, 94
genomes, 10
genotype, 15, 55
Gleevec, 94
GM (genetically modified) crops, 102–104
grasshoppers, sex determination in, 56
guanine, 7, 43, 44, 47

H

haploid cells, 54–55. *See also* gametes
Harvey, William, 17
HD gene, 77–78
hemophilia, 80
heredity
   basic rules of, 34
   defined, 7
   historical theories of, 16–23
heterozygous, defined, 14
HGP (Human Genome Project), 96–97
histones, 13, 50
homologous chromosomes, 52
homozygous, defined, 13–14
honeybees, sex determination in, 56
Human Genome Project (HGP), 96–97
humans
   blood types of, 84–86
   DNA of, 8–9
   sex determination in, 55–56
Huntington's disease (Huntington's chorea), 76–78
hybrids, 23, 68

I

identical twins, 54, 83
in-breeding depression, 23

inherited conditions
  autosomal dominant disorders, 75–78
  autosomal recessive disorders, 71–75
  codominance, 83–86
  pedigrees in study of, 81–83
  X-linked disorders, 78–81
inversions, 66

J
Jacobs, Patricia, 46, 59
jumping genes, 40–43
junk DNA, 9

K
karyotype, 46, 88–89
Klinefelter, Henry, 59
Klinefelter syndrome, 59
Kossel, Albrecht, 43

L
law of segregation, 34
Lejeune, Jérôme, 46, 59
Levene, Phoebus, 43

M
maize, 40–43, 104
malaria, 76
Matthaei, Heinrich, 48
McClintock, Barbara, 40–41
meiosis
  described, 13, 52–54
  errors in, 57
Mendel, Gregor, 24–27, 28, 31, 33–34, 36
Mendel's First Law, 34
Meselson, Matthew, 46
messenger ribonucleic acid (mRNA), 47
metaphase, 50
microchips, DNA, 105–106
Miescher, Johann Friedrich, 43
mitochondrial DNA, 100
mitosis, 50–51

model organisms in research, 41
monohybrid cross, 28
monomer, 48–49
monosomy, 58, 61–62
monosomy, partial, 64
monozygous twins, 54, 83
Morgan, Thomas Hunt, 38
mosaics, 67
mRNA (messenger ribonucleic acid), 47
Muller, Hermann Joseph, 39–40
muscular dystrophy, 80–81
mutagens, 63
mutations, genetic
  carcinogens and, 69
  X-ray radiation and, 39–40

N
nature versus nurture, 82–83
Needham, John, 19–20
Nirenberg, Marshall, 48
noncoding DNA, 9
nondisjunction, 57–58, 71. *See also* monosomy; trisomy
nuclein, 43

O
Ochoa, Severo, 48
oncogenes, 69–70
Origin of Species (Darwin), 82

P
P generation (parental generation), 26
Pallister Killian syndrome, 66–67
pangenes, 23
pangenesis theory, 21–23
parental generation (P generation), 26
partial monosomy, 64
Pasteur, Louis, 20–21
pea plants, 24–27
pedigrees, 81–83

peptides, 49
pharming, 104–105
phenotype, 15
pistils, 24
Pisum sativum, 24–27
plants
  genetically modified, 102–104
  tetraploid, 62
pollination of pea plants, 24, 26
polypeptides. *See* proteins
polyploidy, 62–63
preformation, 22
prophase, 50
protein production, 48–49
proteins, 10
proto-oncogenes, 69
Punnett, Reginald, 27
Punnett squares
  dihybrid cross, 34–37
  monohybrid cross, 27–33
Pythagoras, 16

R
radiation, and genetic mutations, 39–40
RB gene, 70
recessive disorders, autosomal, 71–75
recessive genetic traits, 13–14
recombinant DNA cloning, 100–101
recombination, 52
Redi, Francesco, 18–19
reduction cell division. *See* meiosis
reproductive cloning, 98–100
research. *See* genetic research
retinoblastoma, 70
RNA, messenger (mRNA), 47

S
SCID (severe combined immunodeficiency), 89–95

SCNT (somatic cell nuclear transfer), 100, 102
sea turtles, sex determination in, 56
second filial generation (F_2), 27
selective breeding, 23
severe combined immunodeficiency (SCID), 89–95
sex chromosomes
  in genetic disorders, 46
  and sex determination in humans, 55–56
  trisomies and, 59–61
sex determination, 55–56
Siamese twins, 54
sickle cell disease, 74–75, 76
somatic cell nuclear transfer (SCNT), 100, 102
Spallanzani, Lazzaro, 20
spontaneous generation, 17–21
Stahl, Frank, 46
stamens, 24
start codon, 48–49
stem cells, 93, 101–102
Sturtevant, Alfred, 38
super-conserved regions, 9

T

Tay-Sachs disease, 74, 76–77
TB (tuberculosis), 77
telophase, 50
teratogens, 63
tetraploidy, 62
tetrasomy 12p, 67
therapeutic cloning, 101–102
thymine, 7, 43, 44
titin, 49
Tjio, Joe Hin, 46
transcription, 47
transgenic animals, 104–105
translation, 48
translocations, 64–66, 71
transposable genes, 41–43
transposons, 41–43
triple X syndrome, 61
triplody X syndrome, 61
triploidy, 62
trisomy, 58–61
trisomy 21 (Down syndrome), 46, 57, 58–59, 88–89
tuberculosis (TB), 77
tumor suppressor genes, 69, 70
Turner syndrome, 61–62
turtles, sex determination in, 56
twin studies, 82–83
twins, types of, 54, 83

U

uracil, 47

V

van Leeuwenhoek, Antoni, 17
vector viruses, 93
Vetter, David, 90–91
virus vectors, 93
von Tschermak, Erich, 36

W

watermelons, seedless, 63
Watson, James, 44–46
Wilkins, Maurice, 44

X

X chromosome, inactivation of, 61
X-linked disorders, 78–81
X-ray diffraction, 44
X-ray radiation, and genetic mutations, 39–40
XXX syndrome, 61
XYY syndrome, 59–60

Z

Zech, Lore, 46

About the Author

Kristi Lew is a former high school science teacher with degrees in biochemistry and genetics. After years in the classroom and cytogenetics laboratories, she now owns a professional K–12 educational writing service that specializes in writing nonfiction science books for students and teachers.